THE DYNAMICS
OF RELIGION

Process and Movement in Christian Churches

BRUCE D. REED

Darton, Longman & Todd
London

First published in Great Britain in 1978 by
Darton, Longman & Todd Ltd
89 Lillie Road, London, SW6 1UD

ISBN 0 232 51424 0

Printed in Great Britain by The Anchor Press Ltd and bound by Wm.
Brendon & Son Ltd., both of Tiptree, Essex.

THE DYNAMICS OF RELIGION

Process and Movement in Christian Churches

Bishop Lyttelton
Library
Winchester

Contents

To

Barry Palmer

whose collaboration in clarifying
and expressing the fundamental
thinking intrinsic to this book
enabled it to be published.

Foreword

The following pages set out the reasoning which has led to the formulation of a theory of religion – the oscillation theory. The presentation will be misleading if it leaves the impression of a series of logical steps leading to a final conclusion. It is more accurate to see the theory as evolving from a loose network of assumptions and hypotheses around the theme of human dependence, a theme which we were constantly exploring in a variety of ways – through conferences on the study of human groups, advisory work on the role of clergy and the organisation of religious institutions, field research on the relation of churches to their communities, and practical training and formation of men, women and children for their lives as Christians in churches, homes, work and schools. Only as we related our findings to those of others in the fields of sociology, anthropology and psychology did we begin to perceive that our work might have a useful contribution to make in the wider study of religion.

If I had not been working for an institution among colleagues who were as interested as I was in seeing where our discoveries were leading, I would have given up long ago. We were fortunate in that we were placed in circumstances, first in working for the Christian Teamwork Trust, and then from 1969 for the Grubb Institute, where we had a freedom to select our own areas of research and study if we could get interested sponsors to provide the necessary funds. Only so were we able to engage in such a wide range of activities. Once we had hinted that it seemed we were on to something, as far back as 1968, we found ourselves struggling to meet the expectations of the many friends and interested parties who participated in and who funded different research projects and assignments.

Many attempts at writing proved abortive because we were only too aware of the gaps in our knowledge and reasoning, despite the considerable piles of fieldwork material and research notes. The final shove came in two stages. First, when the Christian Teamwork Trust set up a working party to examine the relevance to the churches of the ideas we had generated in the Grubb Institute; and second when the College of Preachers in Washington DC invited me in 1977 to spend a semester with them as their first International Fellow.

By this time we had concluded that the most important thing was to publish our ideas to enable general discussion of them by others, accepting that there yet remained many elements requiring further unpacking. This book can therefore be seen as a basic introduction to the theory. It is a statement of work in progress and we do not see that we have fully justified or proved anything that is said. A key element in any scientific endeavour in generating hypotheses is not to sit on a theory but expose it for public debate.

Circumstances surrounding the purpose of this essay raise for us questions about its readership. From a scientific standpoint we wanted it to be taken as a contribution to sociological and psychological thinking about society and the function of religion in that setting. However, since the christian churches have provided the milieu and raw material for analysis, if the theory were to prove valid it would present implications for the leaders and membership of those churches who might wish to act on it in a practical manner. By so doing they would be putting the theory to one of its most stringent tests. We accept that what we have written will therefore have a different value depending upon whether the basic discipline of the reader is social psychology or theology or neither of these.

The structure and rationale of the writing is seen in the Table of Contents. But the sequence of chapters exposes a problem which we have as yet failed to resolve. In introducing the theory we have begun from the experience of the individual and from this it might be taken that we consider religion to be the consequence of an extrapolation from *individual* experience. Careful reading will show that this is not so. We seek to show that the primary factor in religion is *corporate* behaviour. The concept of corporateness is fundamental to our thesis and we recognise that we have not investigated this in the depth it demands. We are aware of considerable debate raging around this area; our study of group behaviour provides our point of departure for the development of the concept. This is therefore high on our list for further research, not only from a sociological, but also from a theological standpoint.

Another important concept demanding research is the binary view of human existence (see pp.68ff.). While this, like that of corporateness, is not novel, nor restricted to contemporary western thinking, the establishment of the universality of this view is crucial to the validity of the general religious theory of oscillation.

For the sake of completeness it is worth noting other topics which we expect to explore further, though their significance for the reader will not be apparent before the book itself is read. They include:

the growth of symbols and how different rituals and liturgical forms act as "containers" for the oscillation process;
the relationship of the process to eastern religious behaviour;
the typology of roles of religious leaders from different religions, including primitive religions, with respect to their exercise of authority and power;
the effect of religious behaviour on the maintenance and change of values in a society; and
the current influence of religion on British society and its social institutions.

It is hoped that papers on some of these subjects will be the basis of the next exposition of the theory.

Specifically christian issues include:
an analysis of Church history in the light of the oscillation theory;
the symbolic meaning of the Holy Spirit in relation to the transformation phase of the oscillation process;

the relevance of symbolic language to the search for objective reality and truth; and
the application of the notion of functional religion to the
actual life situation of a church in its local environment.

While I take full responsibility for the ideas, other present
and past colleagues, in addition to Barry Palmer, who have
carried out research which has contributed to the writing of
this book are: David Durston, whose project on "The Task
of the Local Church" was grant-aided by the Sir Maurice
Laing Trusts, the Oak Trust, the Yapp Education and
Research Trust, the Butlins Group Charity Fund, the Diocese
of Chelmsford and the Christian Teamwork Trust; Les
Oglesby, who worked on the project "The Local Church
serving its Neighbourhood" for St Peter's, Eaton Square,
London, sponsored by the parish and augmented by a grant
from the Christian Teamwork Trust; Jean Hutton, who did
most of the fieldwork for the project, "The Rural Deanery,
its Leadership, Tasks and Structures", sponsored by the
Sub-Diocese of Reading and also aided by the Christian
Teamwork Trust; Peggy Welman, who assisted David Durston and myself in the project "Church and Community in the
All Saints' District of Putney", likewise grant-aided by the
Parish of Putney and Christian Teamwork Trust; and John
Bazalgette and Dorothy Berridge, who assisted on the project, "The Human Family and God", grant-aided by the
Marble Arch Trust; and Colin Quine, who engaged in library
research on anthropological and sociological aspects of the
study.

In the initial stages Ken Rice of the Tavistock Institute of
Human Relations pointed up some of the areas to be
explored, and their examination in the churches was encouraged by Richard Herrick, now Provost of Chelmsford
Cathedral.

The writing had to be squeezed in between other assignments in the Institute and this was only possible because
grants were made by the Survey Application Trust and the
New Hall Trust, which enabled both Barry Palmer and
myself to continue our work. St Deiniol's Library and the
Washington College of Preachers provided facilities in which

we could write.

The encouragement and support of the Grubb Institute Council and the Christian Teamwork Trust working party continued throughout, and it was not diminished as they patiently waited for the final version. Gordon Bridge, the Chairman of both groups, placed us in his debt by compiling the index. Our gratitude extends to many secretaries who typed up notes and drafts, and especially to Daphne Miller for struggling through hundreds of pages of my hand-writing.

B.D.R.

PART ONE

Chapter 1

Process and Movement

Religion takes many forms. In this book we concentrate on one manifestation of the religious imperative – the christian religion. Within this tradition we focus upon the activities of the christian churches in Western industrialised countries. Amongst these we give particular consideration to the rites and practices of the churches in England, primarily the Church of England.

This concentration of attention does not imply lack of interest in other forms of religious behaviour: our aim is an understanding of religion as a feature of human life, not of the practices of any particular religion or confession. Our focus reflects the fact that our personal knowledge of this religious form has been a major point of reference in generalising about religious behaviour. Through studying in detail, and reflecting upon, the christian religion as it actually manifests itself in Britain, we hope to be able, not only to provide an analysis which will be of use to believers in this country, but also to offer a model for the interpretation of religious behaviour in any environment.

The feasibility of this larger aim stems from our methodology. We shall interpret religious behaviour, not from the believer's standpoint, but from that of the human sciences – primarily psychology, anthropology and sociology. Our particular theoretical standpoint will become apparent as we proceed. We shall regard the interpretations which believers place upon their own behaviour as one important element in our object of study – as other social scientists have done.

We shall not speak of 'religious experience', as though religiousness was a quality which some experiences have and others do not have. We shall regard the behaviour of men and women in acts of worship, and their experience of participating in such acts, as an aspect of human life which we shall seek to understand in the context of other aspects of human life, political, social, economic, ethical and aesthetic. We shall be interested in the connotations of religious language, but make no assumptions about their denotations – that is, the realities they are believed to refer to. This is a methodological standpoint: it will be evident from time to time that the writer's personal standpoint is not wholly defined by his method.

We work therefore within and between two interpretative frames. The primary frame, for the purposes of this study, is a behavioural or psychological frame. The secondary frame is theological.

Worship observed

Corresponding to these two frames of reference are two key terms which we shall employ: 'process' and 'movement'. To make a start at establishing their meaning, we shall discuss three accounts of traditional christian religious behaviour.

Here first is a brief description of the behaviour of Christians by a pagan writer of the second century, Pliny. He does not share the beliefs of those on whom he is reporting, although he assumes the familiarity of the reader, the Emperor Trajan, with the nature of religious ceremonies:

> They maintained, however, that the amount of their fault or error had been this, that it was their habit on a fixed day to assemble before daylight and recite by turns a form of words to Christ as a god; and that they bound themselves with an oath, not to break their word, and not to deny a deposit when demanded. After that was done, their custom was to depart, and to meet again to take food, but ordinary and harmless food; and even this (they said) they had given up doing after the issue of my edict, by which in accordance with your commands I had forbidden the existence of clubs. On this I considered it the more

necessary to find out from two maidservants who were called deaconesses, and that by torments, how far this was true: but I discovered nothing else than a perverse and extravagant superstition (Epp.XX.96,c.112, quoted in Stevenson, 1957).

Pliny's letter shows considerable perplexity. These people's behaviour is apparently harmless. There are apparently no orgies or other obvious satisfactions for the worshipppers, yet, as he says elsewhere, they are prepared to be executed rather than cease participating in these rites. It may be assumed that they have a meaning to the participants which makes the risk they take worthwhile; yet their account of this rationale is to Pliny unintelligible, a 'perverse and extravagant superstition' concerning an obscure figure referred to as 'Christ'.

Our second example, from Karl Barth, points up the apparent discrepancy between the outward significance of the event of going to church, and the urge of the people to participate:

Here is a building, old or new, of which the very architecture, even apart from the symbols, paintings, and the appointments which adorn it, betrays the fact that it is thought of as a place of extraordinary doings. Here are people, only two or three, perhaps, as sometimes happens in this country, or perhaps even a few hundred, who, impelled by a strange instinct, or will, stream toward this building, where they seek – what? Satisfaction of an old habit? But whence came this old habit? Entertainment and instruction? Very strange entertainment and instruction it is! Edification? So they say, but what is edification? Do they know? Do they really know at all why they are here? In any case, here they are – even though they be shrunk in number to one little old woman, and their being here points to the event that is expected or appears to be expected, or at least if the place be dead and deserted, was once expected here.

After describing the behaviour of a man, the minister, who

by his leadership arouses strange expectations in the worshippers, Barth goes on to say:

> Everyone must apparently, perhaps *nolens volens*, speak of
> God. And then the man will have the congregation sing
> ancient songs full of weird and weighty memories, strange
> ghostly witnesses of the sufferings, struggles, and
> triumphs of the long-departed fathers, all leading to the
> edge of an immeasurable event, all, whether the minister
> and people understand what they are singing or not, full of
> reminiscences of God, always of God. 'God is present!
> God *is* present.' (Barth, 1928, pp. 105f).

Like Pliny, Barth perceives something mysterious about
the behaviour of those who take part in christian worship. He
goes further than Pliny in entering into the experience of the
worshippers, reflecting his own questioning of why a modern congregation should engage in such archaic customs. He
conveys an inkling of the reason why people come to church
in the feeling he builds up round the word 'God', and round
the 'immeasurable event' which is awaited. He also suggests
the possibility that they may be unaware what it is that they
have come for. They satisfy an old habit.

Our third example is based upon the writer's own experience of attending an ordinary Sunday morning service of the
Church of England. The experience of visiting an unfamiliar
church has been chosen deliberately, since this stresses the
variety and range of feelings which arise in the course of such
an event:

> Picture yourself one Sunday morning walking up to a
> church building where you have never been previously.
> You have come to worship God, but you also want to
> remain aware of what is happening to you and around
> you. As you come to the entrance you slow down, you
> probably are uncertain about what will occur inside. Pas-
> sing through the doors into the church itself you feel
> stranded until you have the security of a place to sit. Those
> who welcome you, hand out books or service sheets, are
> warm hands and blurred faces usually split horizontally by

a smile. Looking around you begin to focus more clearly on where you are. The decorations and some of the furniture do not merely grace the spaces, they stand out with symbolic meaning. You notice people's faces; some seem as if they have been pulled into shape, others are nonchalant and casual, others are relaxed and taking things naturally and others are tense with looks of faraway places in their eyes. You try to discover from the books or service sheets what is the routine which will be followed and decide whether you can sit back because the liturgy is familiar, or whether you will have to keep your wits about you and watch those whom you pick out as regular attenders who know their way about. You remain alert in order not to be embarrassed when the service commences. You watch the entrance of the clergy, wondering if they will become real people to you. Depending upon how well you know the order of service and the hymns, you will either be able to take in the meaning of the words or just be grateful you can keep going. In the latter case you may be unaware that you are singing sentiments which you would blush to say, and adding *Amen* to prayers you don't really understand.

The music and words of sacred scripture, creed and sermon are obviously designed to make you think about God. There is generous use of ideas and word-images. The pictures of Father, King, Shepherd, Saviour may evoke feelings of dependence or their oriental impact may even alienate you. But if you are drawn by them and by the concerted movements of the congregation into the attitude of worship you may find out that you are being called upon to become respectively child, subject, sheep and sinner. If you watch those people around you, you may have a problem of associating these emotive roles with such ordinary-looking men and women. If this disturbs your attention you may suddenly wonder what all this has to do with the world outside and whether it has any value for the poor, sick, deprived and oppressed, and speculate if those leaders whom you prayed for will really get any benefit because you spoke about them to God. If you are taking part in a service of Holy Communion you have the oppor-

may also be regarded as related to each other as 'container' and 'contained' (cf. Bion, 1970). The inarticulate human process is given form and consciousness through the theological rationale, which thus contains and moulds it and is vitalised by it.

The first element we shall refer to by the term *process*. This word is at this stage a practically empty term, enabling us to pose the question: what is the nature of the process by which men and women alternate between the activities of everyday life and certain other activities which they interpret to themselves in the language and symbols of religious belief?

The second element we shall refer to by the term *movement*. We shall view religious activities as manifestations of an historical movement, which supplies a rationale or interpretation of the meaning of these activities. The word 'movement' is used here in the same sense as it is used of the Impressionist movement or the suffragette movement. The core of a movement is an emotive idea; in the case of a religious movement, a myth or system of myths.

Since we are concerned with christian churches in Britain, we are taking as our starting point a situation in which the movement is exogenous rather than indigenous. The implications of this will be explored further when we come to discuss folk religion (Chapter 5). In this study we are however not primarily concerned with the origins of the rationale supplied by the movement, so much as with its interaction with the process. The interpretative function of a movement is illustrated by the liturgical *words* which accompany the administration of baptism or Holy Communion; and by Joshua's injunction in the following incident:

> And Joshua set up twelve stones in the midst of the Jordan, in the place where the feet of the priests bearing the ark of the covenant had stood; and they are there to this day.... And he said to the people of Israel, 'When your children ask their fathers in time to come, "What do these stones mean?" then you shall let your children know, "Israel passed over this Jordan on dry ground." For the Lord your God dried up the waters of the Jordan for you until you passed over, as the Lord your God did to the Red

Sea, which he dried up for us until we passed over, so that all the peoples of the earth may know that the hand of the Lord is mighty; that you may fear the Lord your God forever.' (Joshua 4:9,21-24)

Employing the familiar categories of ritual and myth, we may say that ritual is the meeting-point of process and movement. It is the observable phase of a human process, and as such may be interpreted in many different ways, which may be fragmentary, or may have the character of enduring myths. The movement supplies the normative frame of myths and other doctrines, which interpret the ritual and in so doing shape it and are shaped by it.

In the following chapters we shall develop these ideas. More specifically, we shall first of all put forward an analysis of the process, and consider its various manifestations in the worship of the church (Chapters 2 – 5). We shall then seek to demonstrate that the christian movement, in its concepts of the Church and the Kingdom of God, is shaped appropriately to 'contain' the process we have described (Chapter 6). We shall then, in the second part of the book, examine the implications of this analysis for the leadership and organisation of churches, concluding with a personal postscript setting out the writer's own 'action paragraph', based on this study.

Chapter 2

The Process in the Life of the Individual

In introducing the concept of the process, we have so far stated that it manifests itself as the members of a group or community move to and fro between religious activities and the other activities of everyday life. Our task in the next two chapters is to describe the dynamic of this pattern of behaviour.

At the outset it is worth stating that the view of religious behaviour which we shall put forward is fundamentally different from those which associate it with the attainment of a goal. The goal may be to become a better person, to create a better world, to attain a desired level of consciousness or spirituality or, as in Bunyan's *Pilgrim's Progress*, to reach the Celestial City. The path to this goal is seen as difficult, with many pitfalls on the way, as Bunyan describes. The individual, it is supposed, is sustained along the way by his own beliefs, by the support of others, and by spiritual disciplines. His life is therefore one of ups and downs, the struggle lightened by moments or periods of hope, joy and illumination.

Though the language we use is sometimes susceptible of this interpretation, our picture is radically different. It is a view of human life, seen not as a series of events along a line leading to a goal, but as two alternating modes of experience, each with its own way of thinking and its own validity. It should be noted that this is a conception of human life, of which religious activities are one part: it is not itself a description of religion.

The process cannot be understood, or even seen, if one

focusses exclusively upon the individual and his experiences. Nevertheless, the process derives its energy from the function which it fulfills in the life of the individual. For an adequate understanding of the dynamic of the process we therefore turn our attention in this chapter to its manifestation in the life of the individual.

Oscillation

On the 1971 international Everest expedition one of the party, an Indian, was killed in an avalanche. In spite of the hazards involved, and the loss of time, his companions carried his body down below the snowline, to dispose of it, according to the custom of the Hindu religion, by burning it. Having completed this task, they returned to where the disaster had occurred and continued their climb.

From a utilitarian point of view this act was unnecessary, and further endangered the lives of the other members of the expedition. Yet, as far as the members of the party were concerned, it was right and necessary. The incident illustrates, in the lives of a small group of men under extreme conditions, the way in which, in our view, all human beings act from time to time in ways which restore their sense of inhabiting a world of meanings, rather than being objects at the mercy of other objects. Climbing a mountain demands not only physical capabilities. It also demands a secure awareness of the environment as dangerous and unpredictable, but nevertheless presenting conditions which can be observed, interpreted and mastered through the exercise of judgment, skill and courage. Writers and climbers may describe the mountain as hostile, and indeed it may be a partly-conscious wish to attack and defeat the mountain, as though it were a huge ogre, that leads climbers to tackle it. But if the feeling of fighting an implacable and powerful ogre gains the upper hand, then the climbers are likely to lose confidence in their skill and judgment, and to see themselves as helpless specks about to be annihilated. In face of the death of a companion, everyone's meaningful world is threatened with collapse. Only by giving value to the body of the dead companion can the climbers restore their own sense of meaningful endeavour. They reawaken inside themselves the image of a group which cares for them and will mourn for them if they also are killed.

Study of the behaviour of children exploring and learning illustrates, at an earlier stage of development, how adaptation to, and mastery of, the physical and social world, is maintained by periodic disengagement to renew contact with a source of meaning and confidence. John Holt (1967) describes his experience of observing young children with their mothers, and of teaching a young child to swim:

> The courage of little children (and not them alone) rises and falls, like the tide – only the cycles are in minutes, or even seconds. We can see this vividly when we watch infants of two or so walking with their mothers, or playing in a playground or park.
>
> Not long ago I saw this scene in the Public Garden in Boston. The mothers were chatting on a bench while the children roamed around. For a while they would explore boldly and freely, ignoring their mothers. Then, after a while, they would use up their store of courage and confidence, and run back to their mothers' sides, and cling there for a while, as if to recharge their batteries. After a moment or two of this they were ready for more exploring, and so they went out, then came back, and then ventured out again.
>
> In just the same way, this baby in the pool had his times of exploration, and his times of retreat and retrenchment. At times he let me tow him around freely, kicking his feet and paddling his hands. At other times he gripped my arms fiercely, pulled himself towards me, and by his gestures and expression showed me that he wanted to be held in the same tight and enveloping grip with which we had begun. Or he might even ask to go back to the steps, or to be lifted out of the pool altogether. Then, a few minutes later, he would be back in the water and ready for more adventure.
>
> At one time or another I have watched a number of parents trying to teach their very little children to swim. On the whole, they don't get very far, because they are so

insensitive to this rise and fall of courage in the child. Is it because they don't notice? Or because they don't care? Perhaps they feel that the child's feelings are unimportant, to be easily overridden by exhortation and encouragement, or even anger and threats (1970 edition, p. 110).

Holt speaks of filling up the child's 'tank of courage', but we can deduce nothing from this about how contact with an adult changes the child's relationship to the water, so that he is able to have another go at trying to swim in it. We shall consider the mental processes involved later. Holt also indicates how the child's wish to pause and become more babyish for a while is not always understood by adults, who appear to believe in the 'Pilgrim's Progress' model of linear development to a goal to which we referred earlier.

The nature of the behaviour by which children and adults seek periodic access to a source of renewal has been studied extensively by, amongst others, John Bowlby (1969), who refers to it as 'attachment behaviour'. He identifies various forms of attachment behaviour in the very young child: sucking, clinging, following (physically or with the eyes), crying, calling and smiling. Complementary to these are various forms of behaviour on the part of the mother or 'attachment-figure': she checks that he is safe, responds to his crying and smiling, and retrieves him if he wanders too far away. Bowlby demonstrates that attachment behaviour does not disappear as the child grows older, but allows for more extended absences from attachment figures. Periods of attachment normally alternate with periods of autonomous activity in adult life; Bowlby (1969, p. 207) suggests that 'a school or college, a work group, a religious group or political group, can come to constitute for many people a subordinate "attachment-figure", and for some a principal "attachment-figure" '.

It is significant for our thesis here that every form of attachment behaviour, and of the behaviour of the attachment-figure, identified by Bowlby, has its close counterpart in the images of the relationship between Israel (or the worshipper) and God which we find in, for example, the psalms.

The language of the psalms frequently describes the worshipper's distance from, or proximity to, God, as an attachment figure:

But be not far from me, O Lord: thou art my succour, haste thee to help me. (Psalm 22:19)

Yea, though I walk through the valley of the shadow of death, I will fear no evil: for thou art with me; thy rod and thy staff comfort me. (Psalm 23:4)

Nearness to God is often described as feeding upon him, drinking, following him, finding pasture. Crying and calling find a close parallel in supplicatory prayer. The prominent place of prayer in most religions is perhaps the most striking point of contact with Bowlby's observations.

We have used the term 'oscillation' to refer to the alternation of the child and the adult between periods of autonomous activity and periods of physical or symbolic contact with sources of renewal. For most people, the ordering of everyday life provides for regular cycles of oscillation. Each day includes periods when we address ourselves to the problems of living, and periods when we are fed and cared for, relax, reflect and sleep. Similarly, for many, the week and the year provide occasions for more complete disengagement from the problems of living, in the weekend break and the annual holiday. It is onto this base-line, with its regularised opportunities for disengagement, that the oscillation demanded by specific challenges and experiences is superimposed. We have selected illustrations of these occasions which highlight three significant features of the oscillation process: the search for someone or something on whom to depend; the frequent fear of, and resistance to, disengagement and acknowledgement of helplessness, particularly in adults; and the emergence of new ideas and new constructs of the self and the world which take place in the period of disengagement.

The search for someone on whom to depend

The individual's capacity to sustain effective application to the demands of living and pursuing his goals may be threatened either by the difficulty or unpredictability of the environmental conditions (as in mountaineering), or by sickness, injury or other factors which deplete the individual's resources. Sylvia Plath (1956) provides a vivid illustration of oscillation in sickness, and of the feelings which are aroused when a familiar avenue for oscillation to a state of dependence is blocked. She is writing to her mother from Cambridge, England, where she is a Fulbright scholar at Newnham College. While she cannot actually be looked after by her mother, her letter-writing may itself be seen as a form of attachment behaviour:

> ...Every now and then I feel like being 'babied', and most especially now in the midst of a most wet and sloppy cold, which deprived me of a whole night's sleep last night and has utterly ruined today, making me feel aching and powerless, too miserable even to take a nap and too exhausted to read the lightest literature ... Even while I write, I know this too shall pass and some day, eons hence, it may possibly be spring. But I long so much for some sustaining hand, someone to bring me hot broth and tell me they love me even though my nose is ugly and red and I look like hell ... All the nagging frustrations and disappointments that one bears in the normal course of days are maliciously blown up out of all proportion simply because I am not strong enough to cope or be humorous or philosophical: my Venice story came back from *The New Yorker* (and now looks very absurd and sentimental to me). I can't smell, taste, or breathe, or even hear, and these blunted senses shut me off in a little distant island of impotence ... I am being sorry for myself, because there isn't anyone here I can be deeply close to ...

The letter illustrates how the individual's capacity to tolerate ordinary frustrations and disappointments is diminished when she is unable to withdraw to replenish her internal resources. This aspect of oscillation is described in more

technical terms in a detailed study of dependence by Parens
and Saul (1971, p. 132):

> With inner sustainment transiently overtaxed, as by the
> presence of vulnerability-specific stress, the ego reacts
> with fight or flight, often regressing to earlier patterns of
> dependence by turning to external sources for the support
> it transiently does not have from within.

The fear of acknowledging helplessness

As we shall see, the 'regression' referred to by Parens and
Saul may be a way of reducing tension by giving up and
opting out, or a means of *reculer pour mieux sauter*. As the
parents described by Holt illustrate, the rhythm of oscillation
which is natural to children is frequently blocked in adults by
fear of letting go and the shame of acknowledging weakness
or expressing dependence on someone else. Particularly in
Western culture, only the young, the sick and the aged are
permitted to acknowledge need of other people, and even for
them it is more admirable to profess self-reliance. Acknowledging failure or bafflement is equated with what Kahn
(1974, pp. 270ff) has called 'surrender to resourceless dependence', a pit of impotence and disintegration from which in
fantasy there is no return.

The emergence of new constructs

Writers on creativity provide many examples of how scientists and artists have arrived at solutions to the problems they
were struggling with, only when they have abandoned the
struggle. This phenomenon has been referred to as 'regression in the service of the ego' (Kris, 1952). Thus the French
mathematician Poincaré (1908) describes how he discovered a
new class of mathematical functions:

> For fifteen days I strove to prove that there could not be
> any functions like those I have since called Fuchsian func-
> tions. I was then very ignorant; every day I seated myself
> at my work table, stayed an hour or two, tried a great

number of combinations and reached no results. One evening, contrary to my custom, I drank black coffee and could not sleep. Ideas rose in crowds; I felt them collide until pairs interlocked, so to speak, making a stable combination. By the next morning I had established the existence of a class of Fuchsian functions, those which come from the hypergeometric series; I had only to write out the results, which took but a few hours (Vernon (ed.), 1970, p. 81).

In a comparable way, Ernest Newman (1937, p. 390) describes how Wagner arrived at the opening of the Ring cycle, after many years ruminating on the problem:

His difficulty was to begin – to find the tiny point of matter which, introduced into the inchoate fluid of his thinking, would effect in a flash the needed crystallisation. And that tiny point of consolidating matter came to him, unbidden, unanticipated, during his disturbed half-sleep on that hard couch in the hotel at Spezia. Falling into that cataleptic state that is the prime condition for all artistic creation of the highest kind, he suddenly felt, he says, as though he were sinking in a mighty flood of water:

The rush and roar soon took musical shape within my brain as the chord of E flat major, surging incessantly in broken chords: these declared themselves as melodic figurations of increasing motion, yet the pure triad of E flat major never changed, but seemed by its steady persistence to impart infinite significance to the element in which I was sinking. I awoke from my half-sleep in terror, feeling as though the waves were now rushing high above my head. I at once recognised that the orchestral prelude to the *Rhinegold*, which for a long time I must have carried about with me, yet had never been able to fix definitely, had at last come to being in me!

These examples highlight the oscillatory character of creative work. They differ from our earlier examples, in that the problem is handed over, not to another person, but as it were to the unconscious mind, out of which the solution suddenly arises. The experience is frequently described as one of revelation, rather than of decision or discovery. Closer to our interests here are those occasions on which individuals use the actual or imagined presence of another to provide a setting in which they can acknowledge their own weakness and vulnerability, and re-order their view of themselves and their world.

For many people the company of close friends provides the most important occasions when they can talk about themselves and their world unreservedly and become more real to themselves in the process. In a fascinating essay Masud Kahn explores the significance of crucial friendships in the life and work of Montaigne, Rousseau and Freud. He suggests that 'through the presence of God man found for some three thousand years a unique instrument both for relating to himself and objectifying his own nature', and goes on:

> . . . Crucial friendship with the other became exigent only when there was a gap left by the absence of God's presence; and the first example of this is Montaigne's relation to La Boétie in the sixteenth century. It was not necessary for St Augustine to involve himself in a human relationship in order to write his *Confessions*. God was a sufficient witness and object for him to achieve that end. But it was very crucial to Montaigne's invention of the whole genre of essay, and his achievement of his project, that he had this relationship with La Boétie to weave his own narrative of self-experience from . . . (Kahn, 1974, p. 100).

The *Confessions* do indeed illustrate the condition of dependence we are describing. Augustine, writing, we may imagine, alone in his room, addresses God, as One other than himself, apart from whom there is a restlessness that reminds us of the disturbance of Poincaré and Plath described in earlier illustrations:

> Great art Thou, O Lord, and greatly to be praised; great is Thy power, and Thy wisdom infinite. And Thee would

man praise; man, but a particle of Thy creation; man, that bears about him his mortality, the witness of his sin, the witness, that Thou resistest the proud: yet would man praise Thee; he, but a particle of Thy creation. Thou awakest us to delight in Thy praise; for Thou madest us for Thyself, and our heart is restless, until it repose in Thee (1907 edition, p. 1).

In this opening section, Augustine explores the paradoxes of dependence: how can God come into him, who made heaven and earth? How can he enter into God, and repose in him? He then describes his dependence upon his mother as an infant, seeing this as the first manifestation of his dependence upon God:

Thou didst sometime fashion me. Thus there received me the comforts of woman's milk. For neither my mother nor my nurses stored their own breasts for me; but Thou didst bestow the food of my infancy through them ... (1907 edition, p. 4).

Kahn describes how Montaigne had an intense friendship with a man three years older than himself, La Boétie, which was terminated by the latter's sudden death at the age of thirty-three. Eight years later Montaigne 'established a private space in his library at Chateau de Montaigne for himself, and in this space he lived through an extremely devout relationship to an inner presence, which was not that of God, but that of another human being' (Kahn, 1974, p. 102). Kahn stresses that this was not a complete withdrawal, but in our terms one pole of a continuing oscillation; he calls it 'a dialogic process between a withdrawal towards the self in the omnipresence of an internal object, La Boétie, and a rather vivid and sagacious participation in the affairs of his time ...' (p. 101). Kahn sees this as the precursor of the relationship between psychoanalyst and patient which Freud was to evolve three hundred years later.

It is not our intention to argue that the various processes we have described are in every respect the same. We move clumsily through the rich diversity of human experience. We suggest, however, that there is a common element in all those we have described, which links religious behaviour with the 'secular' experiences we have discussed, and which we have referred to as 'oscillation'. As the essay by Kahn indicates, there are also links with the experience of psychotherapy, as conceptualised by a number of writers, and it is to this material that we now turn for more precise meanings for some of the concepts we have been employing.

Oscillation in psychotherapy

A major breakthrough in understanding religious behaviour, and the experiential as well as behavioural aspects of oscillation, came for the writer through an encounter with the work of D. W. Winnicott in the field of psychotherapy. Winnicott has described how the bad experiences of life, particularly those of childhood, can remain as it were frozen inside us, leading in severe cases to what would usually be regarded as mental illness. He suggests that, for most of us, these undigested disasters are 'reached and unfrozen by the various phenomena of ordinary life, namely friendships, nursing during physical illness, poetry, etc.' (Winnicott, 1958, p. 284). In conversation with the writer, he said:

> People who are ill (and we are all ill to some extent) have a drive to cure themselves. Nothing is more important than to do that. This means they experience a great need to feel real, and they only come to feel real by doing something like regression to childhood dependence, to something which can hold them. This may be localised, for example, in the Church or in music (Winnicott, 1969).

Since Winnicott extends the idea of illness to cover everybody, we may take his statement to mean that regression to childhood dependence is a feature of normal life. Only in the case of the severely traumatised does this process require the special conditions of the therapist's consulting room.

This quotation employs two key words, 'regression' and 'dependence', which take us further into the subjective aspect of oscillation, and require elucidation before we continue.

Both are terms referring primarily to states of mind, and only secondarily to the circumstances which give rise to them or the behaviour through which they are expressed.

We use the term regression to refer to transitions in the individual's mental functioning, from the focussed, analytic type of functioning required for adaptation to, or mastery of, his environment, to the unfocussed, symbolic thinking more characteristic of artistic and religious activities. There is a relaxation of the ego-control which for much of our waking life keeps the flux of our fantasies subjugated to the demands of perceiving and responding rationally to the public world which we share with those around us. In the example of the mountaineers, we would use the term to refer to a progressive clouding of their judgment by the belief that they were at the mercy of a malign being who would inevitably destroy them.

The word unfortunately has overtones of pathology and infantile behaviour which have led some writers to question its use or reject it in favour of alternatives when writing about creative processes (*eg* Bettelheim (1967), Ehrenzweig (1967), and also P. M. Turquet, in conversation). We have retained it, both because of its use by Winnicott, and also Kris (1952), Hartmann (1958), and Bion (1961), and because we suspect that the antipathy it arouses is in part a reaction to the process signified, and not just to its misleading associations. Regression may be seen as a re-version, not necessarily to the primitive mentality of the infant, but to the unclouded vision of the child; but in either case the process may be repugnant to the adult mind.

Whether regression is functional or dysfunctional depends upon the circumstances. Here is an example, from a work of fiction (Vonnegut, 1967, p. 37), in which involuntary regression obscures the capacity of the hero, Paul, to enter into an adult relationship with his boss, Kroner:

Kroner's enormous, hairy hand closed about Paul's, and Paul, in spite of himself, felt docile, and loving, and child-like. It was as though Paul stood in the enervating, emasculating presence of his father again. Kroner, his father's closest friend, had always made him feel that way, and seemingly wanted to make him feel that way. Paul had sworn a thousand times to keep his wits about him the next time he met Kroner. But it was a matter beyond his control, and at each meeting, as now, the power and resolve were all in the big hands of the older man.

It will be seen that, in this incident, Paul does not cease to be aware that he and Kroner are adults who have a working relationship; he does not in this sense lose touch with reality. Yet his feelings and behaviour are in part dictated by another image of their relationship, according to which Kroner is his father and he is a little boy. His predominant feelings are therefore of being 'docile, and loving, and childlike', though somewhere inside himself he feels quite the opposite.

In other circumstances, regression is not dysfunctional. If we are to enjoy reading a novel or watching a play, it is necessary for our emotions to be engaged by the events represented. The distinction between the world of reality and the world of the novel softens, and for a while we experience the plight of the hero as though it were our own. Like Paul in the previous example, we do not lose our awareness of our actual circumstances; but in this case the tension between the two worlds we are in is not uncomfortable – unless we are desperately reading the novel to distract ourselves from a pressing problem.

Participation in acts of worship has some parallels with the second example. In worship our thoughts and feelings are engaged by narratives, images and ideas which refer to a world, or a realm of experience, other than that of our working and social lives. For example, let us imagine we sing this hymn (to whatever tune is familiar to the reader):

> Dear Lord and Father of mankind,
> Forgive our foolish ways;
> Reclothe us in our rightful mind;
> In purer lives Thy service find,
> In deeper reverence, praise.
>
> In simple trust like theirs who heard,
> Beside the Syrian sea,

The gracious calling of the Lord,
Let us, like them, without a word
Rise up and follow Thee.

O Sabbath rest by Galilee!
O calm of hills above,
Where Jesus knelt to share with Thee
The silence of eternity,
Interpreted by love!

With that deep hush subduing all
Our words and works that drown
The tender whisper of Thy call,
As noiseless let Thy blessing fall
As fell Thy manna down.

Drop Thy still dews of quietness,
Till all our strivings cease;
Take from our souls the strain and stress,
And let our ordered lives confess
The beauty of Thy peace.

Breathe through the heats of our desire
Thy coolness and Thy balm;
Let sense be dumb, let flesh retire;
Speak through the earthquake, wind, and fire,
O still small voice of calm!

(John Greenleaf Whittier, 1807-1892)

We may sing this hymn and feel only embarrassed by the sound of our own voice, disappointed that the priest or minister has not chosen the tune we know, and worried about whether we remembered to switch the oven onto the automatic timer. Or we may sing it and be moved by it. In this case we may feel, in turn, shame at the pettiness of our lives, confidence in Christ, and longing for the peace and quietness that come from God. We move through several identities without any sense of strangeness: we become the fishermen called by Christ to follow him beside Galilee, the hills around Galilee, Jesus in communion with his Father, the people of Israel receiving manna from heaven, and Elijah hearing the voice of God in the mouth of his cave.

Two types of mental activity

It will be seen that, in both these examples, it is possible to distinguish between two frames of mind or ways of experiencing a world, one which is oriented towards recognising and dealing with present and future realities in the 'public' world, which we have called W-activity, and one which is oriented towards images which may be connected with the public world, but which originate in imagination, 'in the mind', which we have called S-activity. Regression is the process by which S-activity becomes dominant, and W-activity becomes subsidiary or is suppressed altogether.

Several psychologists and behavioural scientists have described these two frames of mind, or patterns of behaviour which appear to correspond to them. On the following pages we list some of the terms used by different writers (Table 1). These paired concepts have a relationship to those in the table of anthropological and other concepts given later (p. 69), but it is not a simple one. This study will indicate how the two classes of concepts are related, as it continues. Within most frames of reference the concepts in the left hand column, in particular those employed by Freud, have associations with infantile, immature or neurotic behaviour. As such they lend themselves to a 'Pilgrim's Progress' view of human development, in which they are progressively left behind as we reach adulthood. For this reason we have in our own Institute preferred to coin our own terms, in the hope that new and unfamiliar expressions will collect to themselves less misleading associations. Our decision to do this found subsequent confirmation when we read Charles Rycroft's critique (1962) of Freud's concepts. Rycroft suggests (to use our terms) that both S-activity and W-activity are integral to normal functioning, with one or the other predominating under different circumstances. Only in neurosis, and under severe stress, do they become dissociated, when S-activity

Table 1. **Binary concepts of mental activity**

S-Activity	W-Activity	This volume
Primary process Unconscious. Displays condensation and displacement, *ie* images tend to become fused and can readily replace and symbolise one another. Uses mobile energy, ignores categories of space and time, governed by the pleasure-principle. Inherently maladaptive, antagonistic to secondary process thinking.	**Secondary process** Conscious. Obeys the laws of grammar and formal logic, uses bound energy, governed by the reality-principle. Develops with adaptation to external world, intimate connexion with verbal thinking.	Freud (1911) Summary from Rycroft (1968)
The libidinal component of adaptation.	The self-preservative component of adaptation.	Rycroft (1962) (See this volume, p. 25)

Presentational symbolism
Mode of mental activity which uses visual and auditory imagery rather than words, presents its constituents simultaneously and not successively, operates imaginatively but is incapable of generalising, has no grammar or syntax, uses elements that derive their meaning from their relations to the other elements simultaneously present and not from any defined or dictionary meaning. Typical examples: music, art, dream, ritual, myth.

Discursive symbolism
Mode of mental activity using symbols presented in a linear order, like beads on a rosary. Relations turned into something like objects. Has vocabulary, syntax, possible to define meanings of single words or other symbols. Has primarily a general reference. Typical example: language.

Langer (1942) and as summarised by Rycroft (1962)

Iconic coding, communication
About relationships, lacking negatives, lacking tense, lacking identification of linguistic mood (*ie* indicative, subjunctive etc.), metaphoric, characteristic of non-verbal communication.

Digital coding, communication
About persons and things, to which predicates are attached, conscious, conventional or arbitrary coding characteristic of verbal language.

Bateson (1973)

Table 1 continued

		As characterised by Laing (1961)
Phantasy Mode of experiencing oneself in relation to others, usually but not necessarily unconscious, involves issues of full/empty, good/bad, destruction/reparation, anxiety/security, experienced primarily in physical terms; firm distinctions between self and other, part and whole, do not hold.	**Apperception** Perception. Evaluation. Insight. (Laing does not discuss apperception in detail. As Bateson says: 'Nobody, to my knowledge, knows anything about secondary process. But it is ordinarily assumed that everybody knows all about it …')	
A–Thinking Term derived from 'autism'. Thinking which is fantasy-dominated, self-generated, uncorrected by reference to external reality; includes fantasy, dreams and nightmares, visionary activity, hypnagogic imagery, hallucinations.	**R–Thinking** Term derived from 'reality'. Prominent in sane, adult wakefulness, in its most logical, realistic and prejudice–free moments; taken to include realistic appraisal in terms of the evidence, critical evaluation, and logical inference of a valid kind.	McKellar (1957)

Basic assumption activity (in groups)	**Work group activity (in groups)**	Bion (1961)
Activities having attributes of powerful emotional drives. Require no training, experience or mental development. Instantaneous, inevitable, instinctive. Make no demands on the individual for a capacity to co-operate; (geared to survival of group as an object of attachment).	Co-operative, voluntary, depends on sophisticated skill developed through years of training. Geared to a task, related to reality. Methods are rational and therefore, in however embryonic a form, scientific.	
Activity of minor brain hemisphere	**Activity of dominant brain hemisphere**	Popper and Eccles (1977, p. 352)
No liaison to consciousness. Almost non-verbal. Musical. Pictorial and pattern sense. Visual similarities. Synthesis over time. Holistic – images. Geometrical and spatial.	Liaison to consciousness. Verbal. Linguistic description. Ideational. Conceptual similarities. Analysis over time. Analysis of detail. Arithmetical and computer-like.	

The descriptions and definitions given are summarised from the works indicated, except in the case of bracketed phrases, which are our own. We do not mean to imply that we regard the terms in each column as exact equivalents: clearly they are not.

may indeed usurp its function and give rise to infantile behaviour.

We propose therefore to use these terms in this study, and to define them in this way:

S-activity is a mode of experiencing which is dominant in dreaming, day-dreaming, artistic creation, artistic appreciation, ceremony and religious activity. It is concerned with value and meaning rather than fact, with what people and things *symbolise* for the individual, rather than with their behaviour and properties in themselves; hence the term S-activity. Its content is emotionally-charged images, or fantasies, which are given conscious form in the above activities, but are generally unconscious when W-activity predominates. S-activity is concerned with people and things in their significance for the survival and well-being of the individual, and in their relatedness to each other and to him. Thus Paul's fantasy of Kroner is of Kroner-for-Paul, and not Kroner-in-himself. S-activity is thus about relatedness: about feeding and being fed, destroying and being destroyed, depending and being depended upon, dominating and submitting, penetrating and being penetrated, filling and being filled, absorbing and being absorbed.

W-activity is a mode of experiencing which, when dominant, characterises all those activities in which we seek to know, understand and modify or adapt to the people, objects, institutions and events around us – activities which may be summarised crudely in the word 'work', from which we have taken the term W-activity. W-activity is concerned with differentiating between objects and understanding a world which is not part of ourselves and cannot be magically known or controlled. Its content is constructs which categorise things as they are, but are always provisional and open to revision in the light of further information or experience.

As we have said, S-activity and W-activity are two elements in the way we experience ourselves and the world, which can be described separately but which operate all the time, in combinations which either complement or obstruct one another. The meaning of the terms cannot be conveyed solely in verbal definitions; we hope that those for whom the above statements are not illuminating will recognise the processes we are referring to in their own experience, through their usage in the following pages.

Dependence

The word 'dependence', like 'regression', has different overtones in different contexts. In all co-operative activity it is necessary for those who are working together to be willing and able to depend upon each other, aware of the possibility of being let down, but without being over-anxious. From time to time it is necessary for us to entrust our money, our health, or even our lives, to bankers, solicitors, dentists, doctors, airline pilots, and many other people. Every day we rely on the services of bus-drivers, milkmen, postmen and shop-keepers, and the staff of the electricity board, the gas board, the water board and other agencies. Only when these services are interrupted do we become aware how much we normally take them for granted.

To take a more dramatic example, John Bowlby (1973, p. 344) describes the conclusions of a small study which was carried out into the personalities of the Apollo astronauts. He writes:

> Although these men tend to be individualists who show a high degree of self-reliance and a clear preference for independent action, all are reported to be 'comfortable when dependence on others is required' and to have a 'capacity to maintain *trust*, in what might seem conditions of *distrust*'. The performance of the crew of Apollo 13, which met with a mishap en route to the moon, is testimony to their capacity to sustain trust. Not only did they maintain their own efficiency in conditions of great danger but they continued to co-operate trustingly and effectively with their companions at the base on earth.

In other contexts the word 'dependence' implies enfeeble-
ment and exaggerated reliance on other people or, in a phrase
like 'drug-dependence', on specific substances. These are the
usual associations of the word 'dependent', so that it is sometimes used almost as a term of abuse. We hope to show that
dependent relationships take many forms, and cannot be
assumed to be either functional or dysfunctional until their
form has been examined.

In his own writings, Winnicott speaks of regression to
dependence and progress towards independence, both as a
process which takes place in psychotherapy, and as a feature
of normal human development.[1] We have found the term
'independence' inadequate, since it implies that it is the opposite of dependence, that dependence is a thing of the past.
Winnicott is explicit that independence is founded upon satisfactory experiences of dependence, upon what he calls a
'good-enough' mother; that the adult capacity to commit
oneself to beliefs and causes presupposes a capacity for 'belief
in', which is established in childhood (Winnicott, 1965) and
that the individual can from time to time regress to overt
dependence, because, or insofar as, he is able to 'cash in' on
his internalised experience of good-enough mothering.

We have therefore coined the term 'extra-dependence',
where 'extra-' means 'outside', to refer to conditions in
which the individual may be inferred to regard himself as
dependent upon a person or object other than himself for
confirmation, protection and sustenance. Correspondingly,
we use the term 'intra-dependence', in place of 'independence' to refer to conditions in which the individual may be
inferred to regard his confirmation, protection and sustenance as in his own hands. The assumption we make is that
these conditions imply dependence upon internal, assimilated
persons or objects, as evidenced by the fact that they are
sustained by oscillation to extra-dependence.

Our definitions refer to conditions of the individual which
may be inferred by someone else; inferred, that is, from his
behaviour, words, or reported feelings. They refer therefore
to how the individual appears to be construing his circumstances, his subjective world, and not to his reliance upon

[1]cf. Lake's dynamic cycle of being (1966, pp. 132ff).

other people or things as we observe it. Thus he may rely in different ways upon public transport to get him to work, upon the milkman for his milk, upon those who man power-stations for his electricity, and so on, but we would not with respect to these outside bodies refer to his condition as 'extra-dependence', unless his behaviour gave evidence of feelings about them, as might be the case for example if they went on strike. When considering intra-dependence the problem is more complicated, since his capacity for self-reliant living may be founded upon an idea of a dependable environment, to which these bodies contribute.

One further elaboration of the concept of extra-dependence is necessary. We distinguish between conditions in which the individual is *aware* of his dependence, and conditions in which he is not. In the development of the infant, Winnicott distinguishes between what he calls 'absolute' dependence, and 'relative' dependence. The new-born infant, it is believed, has no means of knowing about the care he is receiving, and depends totally upon his mother, since he has not yet developed an awareness of his mother as a person distinct from himself, or indeed of any 'not-me' which is distinct from 'me'. This is the condition of absolute dependence. The word 'absolute' is not a superlative: it simply refers to a state in which the infant 'cannot gain control over what is well and what is badly done, but is only in a position to gain profit or suffer disturbance' (Winnicott, 1965, p. 46). Augustine describes it very similarly: 'For then I knew but to suck; to repose in what pleased and cry at what offended my flesh; nothing more.'

From this stage the infant enters the condition of relative dependence, in which he becomes progressively aware of his mother as a separate person, and therefore of his dependence upon her. If she does not come when he needs her, he does not merely suffer disturbance; he *feels* expectant, or anxious, or angry, or deserted. It is a stage in which mothers 'sacrifice a great deal rather than cause distress and indeed produce hatred and disillusionment during this phase of special need' (Winnicott, 1965, p. 88). It is a stage in which the infant progressively learns to wait, and to understand and tolerate delay and loss. This is the character of the extra-dependence articulated in the psalms and in liturgies, in which the wor-shipper's hope and despondency, anticipation and fulfilment, at the absence or presence of God, are contemplated.

Distinctions between similar states of the individual's awareness of relatedness to other objects have been drawn in the study of artistic creativity (Ehrenzweig, 1967, 209ff) and of learning and knowledge (Bion, 1965).

The stimulus to regression

As our previous examples have indicated, regression to extra-dependence is a response to various stimuli. Typically, the situation is one in which the individual feels he no longer has the resources to meet a new challenge, either because of the magnitude of the challenge or the depletion of his own resources. The actual situation may be one which is usually well within his competence, or he may have learned from past experience that he can never cope with situations like this. The situation may be an illness, a bereavement, a failed examination, a mishandled interview, a marred job of work, an insensitive response to a member of his family. It is observed, for example, that people frequently regress to a more childish orientation towards others when they enter upon a new phase of life, as when a child starts at a new school, or an adult leaves his job to go into training for a new career. The temporary regression usually persists until the individual feels more at home in his new surroundings.

On other occasions, which have particular significance in studying religious behaviour, the response occurs at pre-determined times and places. Just as the thoughts of Pavlov's dogs turned to food when they heard a bell rung, so the thoughts of churchgoers turn to God when they hear church bells! As we shall discuss further later, the individual's rhythm of oscillation is partially synchronised with that of others in any group or community.

Opportunities for regression to extra-dependence may also be sought by the individual, consciously or intuitively, in order to find freedom to re-enter and re-examine the experi-ence of the past, particularly the bad experiences which, in

Winnicott's terms, have been 'frozen', because they were at the time too bad to be contemplated.

Whatever the stimulus, the actual regression process may take various forms, which may turn out to be creative or destructive, or merely to maintain the status quo, in the life of the individual. Kris (1952) and Winnicott (1965) use the expression 'regression in the service of the ego' to distinguish creative regression from the less organised process in which the ego is overwhelmed by regression. In a similar way Balint (1968) distinguishes between benign and malignant regression. We have preferred the terms 'creative' and 'defensive', recognising at the same time that we are subsuming a range of complicated and untidy processes under these two headings.

Creative regression to extra-dependence

Creative regression to dependence requires a suitable setting, what Winnicott calls a 'facilitating environment'. In psychotherapy this is provided by the physical setting, and by the attention, understanding and security conveyed by the therapist. In worship also it is conveyed by the surroundings, and by the quality of attention conveyed by those who lead it. In these and other situations, however, creative regression is only possible if the individual, or group of individuals, is able to use the conditions provided. It is necessary for the individual to be able, in the present situation, to 'cash in' on the experiences of good-enough mothering which he has received in the past. He requires unconscious memories of absolute dependence, in order to be able to take the risk, and tolerate the anxieties of, relative dependence. This is perhaps a psychological version of the statement in the *Letter to the Hebrews*, that 'anyone who comes to God must believe that he exists and that he rewards those who search for him' (11:6).

Creative regression to extra-dependence thus entails a conscious act, on the part of the individual, of placing himself in the hands of another, with due appreciation of the risks involved, but with hope derived from satisfactory experience as an infant. It is not a means of escape from stress or danger, but a means of re-entering the disaster area under conditions in which there is freedom not to be defensive. The patient's awareness of risk indicates that he remains in contact with everyday reality, however tenuously, throughout the process of regression and reintegration. However alarming and potentially overwhelming the emotional world into which he enters, he retains somewhere in his mind the knowledge of what he is up to and where he is. Winnicott refers to this unregressed element in the personality as the 'observing ego', which remains identified with the therapist (1958, p. 289).

The outcome of creative regression to extra-dependence is, in the psychotherapy of Winnicott, Balint, and Kahn, a new beginning in which the patient is able to let go of the habitual ways of seeing the world and himself which have constituted his bondage in the past, and to begin to find/construct a new world and a new self, and corresponding new patterns of behaviour. Balint (1968, p. 166) writes of the time when:

> ... the patient can give up, very tentatively at first, his compulsive pattern. Only after that can the patient 'begin anew', that is develop new patterns of object relationship to replace those given up. These new patterns will be less defensive and thus more flexible, offering him more possibility to adapt himself to reality under less tension and friction than hitherto.

The parallels with accounts of religious conversion are striking, and it seems probable that people have sometimes described in religious terms a radical change of self and world which, as far as psychodynamics are concerned, might have been described in terms similar to those of Balint. In each case there is a 'death': the individual loses a self and a world, with all the terror of that experience. Our intention here however is not to assert that the two processes are identical, but to use psychology as a source of concepts which will be of service to us in studying religious behaviour. It would be absurd to ignore the interpretation which Paul, or Augustine, or Wesley, place upon their experience of conversion, as though this made no difference to their subsequent world-view or their subsequent behaviour. We should also not ignore the evi-

dence of the psychoanalytic writers, that those who seek and
sometimes find such a new beginning through a therapeutic
regression are extremely constricted and unhappy people
who, after their new beginning, develop hesitantly and
slowly, and find that they have perhaps most of a lifetime's
experience to catch up, in learning to deal with the demands
of life.

In later chapters we shall be concerned predominantly with
creative regression to dependence as a recurrent element in
the life of human beings, and in particular of worshippers,
and not only with its more dramatic manifestations.

Defensive regression to extra-dependence

From the earliest days of psycho-analysis it has been
known that under certain conditions patients may enter upon
a form of regression, to a primitive state in which they make
increasing demands for attention and gratification which can
never be satisfied. This process is not readily reversible, and
the possibilities for a creative outcome are more uncertain.
The patient reaches an addiction-like state in which he is
terrified of the withdrawal of the care he is receiving. He has
no observing ego who sees the regression as a search for a
new beginning and an enhanced intra-dependence. Whereas
in creative regression the patient is aware that he and the
therapist are engaged in a co-operative venture, defensive
regression leads to temporary states in which the patient is
relieved of all anxiety and the therapist is taken for granted.
This sense of security is highly precarious. Because he has
totally handed over responsibility for his welfare to someone
else, the patient is thrown into a panic when it appears that
the therapist is not fulfilling this function. When someone
deliberately enters a lift in order to descend to the ground
floor he is not thrown into a panic when the lift begins to
move downwards; but if he feels the floor of his living room
begin to give way under his feet he is thrown into a panic,
because the dependability of the floor is something he has
taken for granted.

Kierkegaard (1844) presents a similar picture in his description of man's state of innocence before the Fall:

In this state there is peace and repose; but at the same time there is something different which is not dissension and strife for there is nothing to strive with. What is it then? Nothing. But what effect does nothing produce? It begets dread. This is the profound secret of innocence, that at the same time it is dread (1957 edition, p. 38).

This observation suggests that defensive regression is an impossible attempt to return to the innocence of infancy – a very literal interpretation of the word 'regression'. In contrast, creative regression does not nurse the illusion that there can be a return to the cradle or the womb: whatever new beginning is achieved, the past remains, however transformed. This is why recovery from creative regression is frequently accompanied by anger and mourning, since with his renewed vision the patient recognises more clearly the years and their possibilities which have been wasted in partial living. This mourning is expressed by Augustine in the *Confessions* (1907 edition, p. 227):

Too late came I to love thee, O thou Beauty both so ancient and so fresh, yea too late came I to love thee. And behold, thou wert within me, and I out of myself, where I made search for thee.

Winnicott suggests that the possibilities for a creative outcome of a radical regression to dependence outside the psycho-analytic setting are restricted by the likelihood that these emotions will create a backlash which cannot be contained without specialised help.

Behaviour in the church setting frequently suggests a state of mind related to that resulting from defensive regression. Changes in liturgy or furnishings sometimes arouse abrupt and implacable hostility or profound grief, indicating that these apparently trivial changes have been felt to jeopardise the precarious state of innocence and repose to which the church member has regressed.

Winnicott and Balint also refer to what seems to be a distinct form of defensive regression. Winnicott describes occasions on which patients have withdrawn briefly into a waking sleep or reverie; they have 'switched off'. Some have talked about the fantasies they have had during these periods. They have felt themselves curled up in the womb, or lying in a mother's lap (Winnicott, 1958, p. 256). Whether or not there are day-dreams of this kind, this behaviour suggests a fantasy of reversion to a state in which no attention need be given to maintaining relations with other people or with the immediate environment. It is taken for granted that the individual is safe. There are thus echoes of Winnicott's state of absolute dependence.

Winnicott found that if, when such a withdrawn state appeared, he could effectively 'catch' the patient, by a comment which showed understanding of the patient's state of mind, contact was established with the regression, which became creative, with potentiality for growth. Usually, however, he writes: ' ... the withdrawn state is not profitable, and when the patient recovers ... he or she is not changed' (Winnicott, 1958, p. 261).

As we have indicated, both religious and secular activities are sometimes used for this kind of brief withdrawal from the pressures of living. John Updike (1968) provides a fictional example of participation in a church service which closely parallels Winnicott's account of withdrawal:

> On command, Piet sat and prayed. Prayer was an unsteady state of mind for him. When it worked, he seemed, for intermittent moments, to be in the farthest corner of a deep burrow, a small endearing hairy animal curled up as if to hibernate. In this condition he felt close to a massive warm secret, like the heart of lava at the earth's core. His existence for a second seemed to evade decay.

Beyond psychotherapy

In this account of the oscillation process we have restricted ourselves so far to its manifestation in psychotherapy, in which the individual seeks to re-order his basic mode of construing the world and himself in it. We have not seen many comparable studies of the way in which he evolves and re-orders the more sophisticated constructs by which he construes the inter-locking sub-worlds of family, school, work, local community, state and international community, and the roles through which he is related to them. Our thesis is that each of these self-worlds is maintained and developed through processes of oscillation.

The subject is considered by Erikson, whose account of human development considers the role of other agencies besides Winnicott's good-enough mother. Winnicott, as we have seen, regards the mother as providing the 'facilitating environment' required for the growth of the infant. Using Hartmann's equivalent term, 'average expectable environment', Erikson (1968, p. 222) suggests that the individual:

> ... calls not only for one basic environment, but for a whole sequence of 'expectable' environments, for as the child adapts in spurts and stages he has a claim, at any given stage reached, to the next 'average expectable environment'. In other words, the human environment as a whole must permit and safeguard a series of more or less discontinuous and yet culturally and psychologically consistent developments, each extending further along the radius of expanding life tasks'.

Our own work, in the study of groups and organisations, and of the place of religious institutions in a community, suggests that every context in which the individual takes up a role constitutes for him an environment which, insofar as it is adequately 'expectable', or 'good-enough', provides occasions in which he can regress to extra-dependence, and in so doing renew and reorder his construct of his relatedness to that environment. Oscillation is not therefore related only to the maintenance of basic identity; it is also the process by which the individual maintains his sense of home, workplace, community and nation as expectable environments. It is to the process of oscillation in these environments that we now turn.

Chapter 3

The Process in Group, Institution and Community

The picture of the life of the individual which we have built up is one of periods of engagement with various tasks, alternating with periods of disengagement which may be creative, defensive, or simply periods of rest. We have called this alternating process 'oscillation'. We have also suggested that each world in which the individual moves – his home, his job, his local community, for example – offers occasions in which he has the opportunity to renew and reorder the way he construes that world and his place in it. They provide opportunities for him to regress to extra-dependence upon figures or objects which are representative of that group, institution or society. What are these occasions?

In many institutions (using this as the generic term for the sake of brevity) they go unrecognised, but they may be identified by their ritual element. Ritual behaviour comprises words and actions which are symbolic rather than utilitarian. They may take their form from utilitarian acts like washing (as in baptism) or eating and drinking (as in the Eucharist), but in this respect the utility is unimportant and may be demonstrably inadequate. They are not however purposeless. They awaken and make manifest ideas about relatedness: the relatedness of persons to each other, to the institution to which they belong, to others outside it, and to God or gods. They express thinking in which, in the terms introduced in the previous chapter, S-activity is overt and W-activity has become latent.

Thus families have their meal-time rituals and their ritual family gatherings. Organisations have their formal occasions, like school assemblies, annual conferences, regimental parades and inspections, weekly staff meetings and daily ward-rounds. All have some actual or vestigial utilitarian function, but in each case what people do, and the significance with which their actions are invested, goes beyond this function. A prison governor described a regular meeting of the senior staff of his prison which was known to everyone as the knitting circle. As the name indicated, they did not seem to make many decisions; it was a time to sit round and chat. Yet no one could seriously contemplate abolishing the meeting. It made more sense to him to suppose that it was a ritual, the function of which was to enable the staff to hold in their minds an idea of the institution and its management as a totality, when they were carrying out their responsibilities in different parts of the establishment.

The life of many institutions may be observed to include ritual occasions of this kind. Activities which appear aimless, ineffective or repetitive become meaningful if it is assumed that they serve to remind people of the nature of the institution they are in, what its aims and values are, who its key figures are (past, present or future), and what is their own status in it. We have reached the conclusion that such occasions are essential for the coherence of any institution. If no such occasions are observed, there is reason to doubt whether the institution holds together as a totality in the minds of its members. For example, it appears to be difficult for pupils or staff in a large secondary school to experience it as a totality, without a daily assembly or some equivalent event.

Implicit in this interpretation of behaviour in institutions is a theory about what institutions *are* (cf. Berger and Luckmann's theory of what constitutes reality for any individual, 1963). Institutions are not physical objects. They are constituted by ideas held in the minds of men and women. Victoria Station is a building in a concentration of buildings called London, but British Rail is a complex idea, held roughly in common by a large number of people, which is held to manifest itself in a variety of persons, occasions, vehicles, buildings and other objects. The core of the idea is constant: it is an institution providing rail services in Britain. The periphery of the idea – the punctuality of its trains, the courtesy of its staff, the range of transport it offers – are subject to revision in the light of continuing experience.

An institution is thus constituted by a shared idea, held in the minds of individuals, whose idea includes a reference to their own position with respect to the institution, as members or non-members, owners, employees, consumers, competitors or merely observers. Whilst institutions are constituted by ideas, this does not mean that they are hallucinations which are dismissed as easily as the court of the Queen of Hearts in *Alice in Wonderland*. They impinge upon us through the behaviour of those who hold them to exist, and on occasions through the agents of laws which legitimate their existence. My knowledge that British Rail is constituted by ideas in people's minds does not prevent me from being arrested if I travel without paying my fare.

Ideas do however fade, and the shared ideas which constitute institutions have to be reinforced, repaired and updated. This requires occasions on which they are not taken for granted, but become the focus of attention. One such occasion is the ritual occasion which we have been examining. These occasions, as we have seen, provide opportunities for the individual to oscillate between intra- and extra-dependence. If we shift our focus to the institution, we become aware of a process by which the idea of the institution is alternately taken for granted and the focus of attention, alternately tacit and explicit, alternately the ground and the figure. This is in fact what we have referred to as 'the process' in this study.

So far however our account of oscillation in an institutional setting has said little about ritual occasions as manifestations of extra-dependence. Our understanding of this aspect of the life of complex institutions is derived in part from the study of smaller and less complex groupings assembled for the purpose of learning about group behaviour. One of the pioneers in this field of study is Wilfred Bion. In conversation with the writer, Bion summed up some of his earlier published observations (1961) in the statement that whenever a group forms it begins to develop its own religion. Our own experience, both in the specially constructed setting of group relations conferences, and in working groups in various institutions, including our own, endorses it; again and again people speak and behave as though their group, their institution, their leaders or their ideas had super-human qualities.

Bion describes many episodes in the life of therapeutic groups in which he appeared to be invested with exaggerated powers. In one such episode (1961, p. 147) he finds himself involved in a transient group religion, first as its deity and then as a blasphemer against the deity:

> Three women and two men were present. The group had on a previous occasion shown signs of work-group function directed towards curing the disability of its members; on this occasion they might be supposed to have reacted from this with despair, placing all their reliance on me to sort out their difficulties while they contented themselves with individually posing questions to which I was to provide the answers. One woman had brought some chocolate, which she diffidently invited her right-hand neighbour, another woman, to share. One man was eating a sandwich. A graduate in philosophy, who had in earlier sessions told the group he had no belief in God, and no religion, sat silent, as indeed he often did, until one of the women with a touch of acerbity in her tone, remarked that he had asked no questions. He replied, 'I do not need to talk because I know that I only have to come here long enough and all my questions will be answered without my having to do anything.'
>
> I then said that I had become a kind of group deity; that the questions were directed to me as one who knew the answers without need to resort to work, that the eating was part of a manipulation of the group to give substance to a belief they wished to preserve about me, and that the philosopher's reply indicated a disbelief in the efficacy of prayer but seemed otherwise to belie earlier statements he had made about his disbelief in God. When I began my interpretation I was not only convinced of its truth but felt no doubt that I could convince the others by confrontation with the mass of material – only some of which I can convey in this printed account. By the time I had finished speaking I felt I had committed some kind of gaffe; I was

surrounded by blank looks; the evidence had disappeared. After a time, the man, who had finished his sandwich and placed the carefully folded paper in his pocket, looked round the room, eyebrows slightly raised, interrogation in his glance. A woman looked tensely at me, another with hands folded gazed meditatively at the floor. In me a conviction began to harden that I had been guilty of blasphemy in a group of true believers. The second man, with elbow draped over the back of his chair, played with his fingers. The woman who was eating, hurriedly swallowed the last of her chocolate. I now interpreted that I had become a very bad person, casting doubts on the group deity, but that this had been followed by an increase of anxiety and guilt as the group had failed to dissociate itself from the impiety.

Similar behaviour has been described by others working in the group dynamics field, usually in an educational rather than a therapeutic setting. Slater (1966) describes how participants in training groups referred to the leader as 'the great stone face', as a 'brooding, inscrutable deity', as 'the Delphic Oracle' or 'Zeus hurling thunderbolts'. They also constructed myths to give purpose to the group and to the leader's failure, as they saw it, to intervene and take charge of the proceedings (Slater, 1966, pp. 12f):

Training groups have difficulty in accepting the idea of an unprogrammed existence. They react with dread to the realization that nothing will happen unless they make it happen – that they are literally being left to their own devices, that there are no rules, no plan, no restraints, no explicit goals. They construct myths which serve to deny the frightening responsibility and aloneness which this state of affairs confers upon them.

The most common, the most pervasive, the most elaborated of these myths is the notion that the entire group experience is some kind of complicated scientific experiment. This takes many forms – sometimes it is seen as a stress experiment, sometimes as a stealthy personality test, or more often simply as a laboratory study of group development – but all varieties have two themes in common: (1) that the goal of the group leader is acquisitive and inquisitive rather than didactic or therapeutic, and (2) that the situation is not under the members' control – that they are helpless pawns in an unknown and unknowable game. Every occurrence is seen as a calculated experimental intervention. A visitor is a 'plant', a leader's illness is a 'test', objects left behind, chairs disarranged by previous occupants of the room, external noises, disturbances, or intrusions are all 'gimmicks' to 'see how we would react'. These interpretations are thus comparable to religious visions and other paranoid 'insights'.

Often conjoined with the experiment myth, but sometimes occurring independently, is the myth of Inevitable Evolution or Universal Utility: the idea that everything taking place in the group, no matter how trivial, frivolous, tedious, and repetitive it may seem, is an essential and anticipated aspect of the group's development. This myth is equivalent to religious explanations of 'evil'. Since group leaders usually perceive more order and meaning in the interaction than do other members, they contribute heavily to the formation of this myth.

Groups of this kind are of course set up to allow processes of this kind to develop, so that they can be experienced and recognised by the participants. In ordinary meetings people's implied assumptions are seldom put into words in this way, but the assumptions can be very similar. An Anglican curate described how he had been responsible for a weekly evening meeting in the crypt of his church, at which visiting speakers were invited to lecture on cultural and religious subjects. One evening during the meeting a woman fainted. People on either side of her drew back and looked expectantly at the curate. Although he had no clear idea of what should be done in such circumstances, he did his best to revive the woman and eventually with help assisted her outside into the fresh air. It was only subsequently that he recalled that over half of those present were doctors and nurses from London hospitals. Although many of those in the meeting were better equipped than he was to give the aid required, their unconscious assumptions about the meeting were such that only the leader of the meeting, the priest, was seen as competent to handle the crisis. He of course endorsed their assumptions by failing to enquire, in the time-honoured formula, whether there was a doctor in the house.

The common factor in these episodes is that the behaviour of the members of the group in question cannot be accounted for solely as rational responses to a realistically perceived situation – that is, as manifestations of W-activity. Bion suggested that such behaviour becomes intelligible if it is supposed that it springs from a shared belief or 'basic assumption', which is usually unconscious, and which is held in common by members of the group. He identified three basic assumptions which occur repeatedly in various forms. Each is an assumption about the group as an object on which the survival of the individual depends, and is in our terms a form of S-activity. One of these assumptions was called by Bion basic assumption *dependence* (for a brief account of three basic assumptions, see Appendix).

When this assumption is dominant, people speak and behave as though the security and well-being of the group, and hence of themselves, stems from one all-providing individual, institution or idea. This 'primal object', as we shall call it, is expected to provide the group with sustenance and protection, without its members having to do anything except wait and receive – the attitude which the graduate in philosophy expressed so precisely in the first example. The members of the group are deprived of all skill, like the doctors and nurses in the last example. They feel themselves to be weak, ignorant, and vulnerable. Initially they may welcome the opportunity to divest themselves of the responsibility and consequent anxiety that goes with knowledge and skill. Later they may resent their impotent condition, without being able to break out of it. Accounts of groups dominated by this type of thinking (*eg* Reed and Palmer, 1972a, Turquet, 1974) present striking parallels with historical and literary accounts of relations between leaders and followers.

We should note two features of these findings. First, in the group situations described, the fantasies of dependence inhibit effective engagement with current tasks. The participants regress to extra-dependence, in circumstances where intra-dependence is required. This observation led Bion, as we shall see later, to conclude that in Western society we localise the expression of the emotions associated with extra-dependence in churches, so that people can think realistically about the demands of life in other areas of society.

Secondly, people speak and act *as though* they believed they had access to an omnipotent being, but they would not consciously affirm such a belief. The primal object is an unconscious fantasy. In the groups we have described some participants come to recognise the influence of such fantasies upon their own behaviour and that of others; in which case they discover a discrepancy between their conscious beliefs about the fallibility of human beings (W-activity), and their unconscious fantasies of beings with super-human powers (S-activity).

When we turn our attention to life in society, we once again discover occasions when people speak and act as though they had access to super-human beings. People talk as though their small organisations could change the world; as though their boss knew everything without being told; as though their group were blameless of the failures, self-interest and limitations of competence which are inevitable in any group. Members of families give presents to 'the best Mum in the world', and people at the last night of the London Promenade Concerts proclaim with great gusto that 'Britannia rules the waves'. We have seen an account in a local newspaper of a woman who recovered from an illness on the day the Queen visited her borough during the Jubilee celebrations, which was clearly playing on the reader's wish to believe that this was some kind of miracle.

These fantasies of extra-dependence do not usually interfere with rational thinking about current tasks. People are for the most part aware that they are conveying an emotional reality, something about the quality of their relatedness to their mother, group or country, rather than describing it objectively. When a nation seeks to force its belief in itself as the best nation upon other nations, this can of course have disastrous consequences. But, if our concept of oscillation is sound, many of these occasions have a benign function.

Having confirmed our relatedness to good and powerful parents, groups and nations, we internalise these links and return to the work of living with renewed morale.

However, some of the beliefs we have mentioned *are* consciously affirmed. The fantasy that the Queen has worked a miracle teeters on the brink of becoming a belief that the Queen has worked a miracle. The sentiments expressed by the promenaders do not tally with the facts about the present strength of the Royal Navy, but they are the best words and music available to express what they *feel* at that moment. Thus the ephemeral fantasies of extra-dependence which have been observed in experimental small groups, and which Bion identified as a group religion, become more substantial in longer-lived groups, institutions and nations. All these are however only glimpses of a phenomenon which takes its most sophisticated form in religious institutions and religious behaviour. It is to this that we now turn.

The process in society: religion

Implicit in this discussion is the idea that for any group to function, and to be experienced by its constituents as a group rather than as a chaotic aggregate of individuals, it requires some kind of bonding, and that this bonding is provided by the *synchronisation* of the oscillation processes of its members. Where we encounter a social group, of whatever size, we can expect to find some consensus, explicit or implicit, about the places, times and ceremonies at and through which its members can together regress to extra-dependence.

The size of the group clearly limits the extent to which its members can gather in the same place. In a small tribe, as anthropologists have observed, it is possible for all its members to participate, at least as onlookers, in its ritual occasions. Observation of such tribes led Victor Turner (1974, p. 193) to conclude that 'society seems to be a process rather than a thing – a dialectical process with successive phases of structure and *communitas*. There would seem to be … a human need to participate in both modalities'. In a populous nation dispersed over thousands of square miles, the processes through which its members retain their sense of belonging to one nation are necessarily more complex. Even on this scale, there are occasions when the whole nation seems to be suspended in extra-dependence, as for example, in Britain on the occasions of the funerals of George VI and Winston Churchill.

These occasions are however exceptional. More significant is the structure of times and occasions which shapes the social oscillation process – for example, when it is time to work and when to rest. Without this, national life would be impossible. A developed form of this is seen in the weekly cycle of life we have today in our society.

The link between oscillation and religion can be stated by saying that religion is a corporate activity which provides a ritual setting for one of the modes of the oscillation process, the extra-dependent mode, and thereby 'binds together' the lives of those who participate in it. We should note that one of the Latin roots of 'religion' signifies 'to bind'[1]; an early christian example of which is the binding together of a religious community by vows. The alternative to religion doing the 'binding' is an acknowledged event co-ordinating activity around the mode of intra-dependence. In agricultural regions this has sometimes been achieved through the institution of the market day. In ancient Roman times this had more significance than religious occasions. In rural England market days and religious festivals have been equally important.

Participation in such corporate activity involves endorsement, by an individual or group, of the process of which they are a part. In religion the mode on which the group focuses is one in which they seek sanction or strength for their lives from outside themselves; it is an extra-dependent mode. The essence of this corporate activity is that the participants express dependence on someone or something of which they have a corporate or shared view, attaching themselves emotionally to that 'primal object'. Hence we may define religi-

---

[1] Cf Max Weber (1966 edition, p. 11): 'The authentic Roman religion contained ... a conception of the impersonal as having an inner relationship to the objectively rational. The *religio* of the Roman surrounded his entire daily life and his every act with the casuistry of a sacred law ... Every fact and indeed every specific element of an act stood under the influence of specific *numina* (spirits).'

ous behaviour as: the behaviour of people, either individually or collectively, which represents (symbolically) dependence on some idea, thing or person, the implied nature and power of which is not wholly susceptible to rational explanation.

Religion provides a focus for behaviour in the extra-dependent mode of the oscillation process. In the intra-dependent mode people scatter through all the diverse institutions of society, engaging in food production, government, education, protection of person and state, home management, creative arts and sciences, and so on. Values attributed to the primal object in extra-dependence are externalised in intra-dependence so that they provide rules for social behaviour. Here we touch upon the question of morality, which classifies behaviour as right or wrong for society, but not necessarily as good or bad for the individual. Referring back to our earlier distinction between process and movement, we can see that it is only when the movement pervades the entire society in which the process is dominant that immorality is equated with sin against God. So long as the leaders of a religion show they have this influence, people will tend to make no distinction between sin and immorality.

Participants in religious acts externalise their dependence through symbols which are incorporated into rituals and ceremonies. These rituals and ceremonies then become means of reinforcing the corporate activity. In some religions the corporate activity is manifested in assemblies for worship (that is, in collective activity) because individuals become attached not only to the primal object, but also to one another. This is something we take for granted in Christianity, but which is also evident in other historic religions such as Islam and Judaism. Sikhism and Bahai also follow this pattern. There is evidence that the Eastern religions, as they adapt to the Western culture in Britain, are practising the same rituals. In most other religions the shared rhythm of oscillation creates such a dominant culture that outward collective activity only occurs infrequently on special occasions. The corporate activity is more frequently expressed individually in, for example, Hinduism and Buddhism in India, Burma and Sri Lanka, where the philosophical idea of the divine with its countless manifestations gives rise to quite different religious behaviour, one instance of which is the emphasis on meditation.

One symbolic action to which religion gives rise is the observation of sacred time; that is, of periods which ritualise the complex and varying oscillation patterns of the members of a society. Such cycles are found in all societies. They may reflect the cyclic movements of sun and moon and the transitions of human life, such as birth, puberty, marriage and death. By ritualising the turning points, such as the winter solstice and the new moon, meaning is given to the remainder of the cycle. These periods supplied the major religious festivals for much of the ancient Near East. Perhaps this is why some people feel that if they have been to worship on the christian version of the winter solstice on Christmas Day, they have done their duty for the year.

We therefore propose this working definition of religion:

> Religion is a social institution which provides
> a setting in ritual for the regulation of
> oscillation processes in a social grouping.

(Without going into much greater detail we can only suggest that it is the religious mode of the oscillation process which effects the synchronisation of the process. Compare Durkheim, quoted by Berger (1967), who states that religion is 'the symbolic representation of integration'. Also Mol (1976): 'Religion is the sacralisation of identity').

If religion concentrates on one mode of the oscillation process, what is its relation to the other mode? When individuals or groups believe there is a primal object which is dependable, to which they can turn in times of distress, then they are willing on other occasions to take risks and engage in change and in exploring the unknown. If religion therefore is able to be sufficiently dependable, the members of a community are supported sufficiently for them to work individually and together in the many and varied conditions of their environment, to produce a social structure which satisfies their collective needs.

The dependability of a religion is closely related to the nature and character which is attributed to its primal object.

Conversely, the nature and character attributed to the primal object influences behaviour in society, in the intra-dependent mode, insofar as, in the other mode, the worshippers have ritually identified themselves with their god, and been infused with the values which are embodied in his character, and with his power to realise these values in action. Therefore if the Christian is worshipping his god with integrity we would expect his life to manifest the qualities of love, justice and righteousness, because these are the characteristics he attributes to divinity.

At the corporate level, integrity demands that these qualities of the primal object are incorporated in the laws of the State. For example we believe that the significance of a religion to a nation can be judged by the extent to which the State is able to ensure the optimum match between its resources and the needs of all its members. So if a State is dominated by one particular social class, then the value say of divine universality has not been adequately realised at the political level. We can attribute this discrepancy to a number of things: first, that a group (the class) has taken over those who lead the rituals and undermined their integrity; second, that the ruling class has a conception of the primal object which suppresses any other conceptions such as those embodied in sacred writing such as the Bible; and thirdly, that religion has become impotent to change the status quo, because the regression to extra-dependence it induces is not a creative regression but a withdrawal which does not allow development or growth.

Types of oscillation

If the whole of any coherent social group is in some way involved in the process without all its members having to take part in religious acts, what is the function of its religious institutions and those who take part in its activities?

Our first clue to this question was provided by some speculative ideas put forward by Bion, arising out of the studies of small groups which we have described. He observed how small groups can become caught up in fantasies of dependence upon all-powerful, all-knowing figures, which engender strong cohesion but which immobilise the group from carrying out the work for which they had come together. The need to find security through regressing to extra-dependence undermines the intra-dependence necessary to engage resourcefully in a task. What prevents society as a whole from being immobilised by the emotions and fantasies associated with the state of extra-dependence? Thinking in particular of the Western world, Bion (1961, pp. 156ff.) suggested that societies 'bud off' religious institutions – that is, churches – to contain or localise the expression of these emotions, so that other institutions are free to go about their tasks in a realistic way. He does not say how this 'budding off' takes place, nor does he make any reference to people moving between the activities of churches and of other institutions. Nevertheless this rather strange idea was important to us, because it helped us to shift our frame of reference from the behaviour of individuals to social processes. It also suggested to us that those who participate in the activities of religious institutions might do so on behalf of others who seldom or never attend a place of worship.

We have since come to the conclusion that it is useful to divide members of any community into three types. There are first those who engage in what we describe as *personal oscillation*. These participate regularly in acts of worship; collectively they experience the process of oscillation for themselves, and are often aware of the point of transition from extra-dependence to intra-dependence as they engage in the various rituals of the church.

The second type are those who engage in *representative oscillation*. These seldom or never attend worship but it is important for them that a member of their family, an acquaintance, or a significant person in the community such as their doctor, goes to church as it were on their behalf. They become anxious if that person does not go, and even if they apparently criticise them for being too religious, it is done in such a way that the churchgoer is reinforced in his behaviour.

A study of the task of the local church carried out by the Grubb Institute provided many examples of representative oscillation. For example, a colleague who carried out the field-work wrote in his notes:

A sidesman told me that after the Sunday morning service he used to go into the public house near the church for a drink with some friends. They often used to ask him if he had been to church and to joke about it. As he told me about this I gained the impression that he would have found it quite embarrassing to go in and tell them he had not been to church. He seemed to feel under some pressure from them to continue to attend church, as if they found some satisfaction in his doing so (Durston, 1972).

Another example may be seen in this account by an Anglican vicar of an East London church who described what happens when an unwitting representative does not go to church. During a Sunday evening discussion an elderly lady in the congregation said how surprised she had been when a neighbour had told her she was sorry she had been ill. She had not been ill, and discovered in the ensuing conversation that her neighbour had jumped to this conclusion because she had not seen her going to church the previous Sunday. Later in the week several others had asked her whether anything had happened to her. She was amazed that people who did not go to church themselves should bother to notice whether she went or not.

As she reflected further, she realised that she often used to see people standing in their windows on Sunday, watching her walking down the road. There were others she used to meet because they were in their gardens as she walked by. By going to church regularly it appears that she had become a dependable element in the worlds of her neighbours. When she failed to appear, they had to supply reasons.

The third type are those who engage in *vicarious oscillation*. This group do not identify themselves with any individual worshipper, but it is important for them that church buildings should remain standing, that they hear the church bells ringing, and that they see people going to church. This group have no apparent interest in church-going, but our studies have indicated that they constitute a considerable group in society which may not be made manifest until the church building is threatened with closure. For many of them, the church is a place to stay away from, but upon which they covertly depend, like the adolescent who apparently abandons his parents when he runs away from home, but likes to think they are still there if he should ever want to come back to them.

An example of this type is seen in the following paragraphs from the study mentioned earlier. The place is Baldock, a small market town forty miles north of London:

> The thirteenth century parish church is near the centre of the town, and the clock in the church tower is visible from many parts of the town. A few years ago it became increasingly difficult to find reliable people to wind the clock, so that it frequently stopped. This aroused considerable irritation in the town, and strong feelings were expressed to the Rector and Churchwardens. Several people said to me with emphasis: 'We did miss it', characteristically using the plural, suggesting they were aware this was a corporate and not an individual feeling. Some described how they used to look at the clock every time they walked down the street from their homes, and from their descriptions it was clear that this was not because they wanted to know the time, but that they were reassuring themselves that the church was still there and the clock still going, so that when they found it had stopped they experienced a sense of deprivation.
>
> When the Rector became aware of the strength of feeling in the town he suggested to the Chairman of the District Council that they should launch a joint fund for the electrification of the mechanism of the clock. A Gift Day and Spring Fair aroused a great deal of interest in the town, with contributions from different organisations such as the Scouts, the Round Table, the Floral Arrangement Society and the Football Club. The sum raised exceeded everybody's expectations, and the surplus beyond what was needed for electrification enabled floodlights to be installed so that the tower is floodlit at night (Durston, 1972).

Such evidence of this third type of oscillation provides a further clue to the place of religion in society. We suggested earlier that every social grouping evolves or develops its own religion. In relatively unsophisticated societies all members of the society may take part in specific religious activities. This evidence indicates the way in which members of more developed societies engage in the process of oscillation without directly participating in religious ritual.

Welfare and development

We have argued that the actions of men and women which are carried out in intra-dependence, in the political, economic, and other areas of society, are based on values which are tested and renewed in extra-dependence. This suggests that a major way of classifying religious behaviour is in terms of its effects on society, and how far these are beneficial or damaging for that society.

Any such assessments are likely to raise questions about the assumptions that are being made about what is beneficial and what is harmful for that society. In order to provide some criteria for examining such assumptions we are drawing on the work of the social scientist Eric Trist, in his study of the transition of society from industrialism to the post-industrial state (Emery and Trist, 1973). Trist uses an open systems approach to organisations and societies, examining the exchanges between the system and its environment which enable the system to survive. He suggests that in examining the results of these exchanges for the system, two variables must be considered, welfare and development.

He defines *welfare*, or well-being, as referring to states of a system under conditions which maintain the steady state. The system remains stable and functions well. Its opposite is ill-fare, or ill-being, which refers to states in which the system still exists, but cannot maintain its steady state. In other words, it is either running down or it is moving towards some explosion. Hence this concept of welfare is about the stability of a system: is it able to maintain a stable state, despite any variations which occur in the environment?

Then Trist defines *development*, or progression, as referring to processes by which a system reaches a higher order of steady states of a more adaptive nature. Its opposite, deterioration or retrogression, refers to processes by which the system reverts to lower order states, which may be either stable or unstable, and which are maladaptive to changes in the environment. Through activities promoting development, a system does not merely rely on the activities through which at present it may be able to survive and maintain a steady state, but modifies itself in one direction or another to greater sophistication, so that it is equipped to deal with a wider range of challenges to its survival and stability.

In developing his argument, Trist maintains that society, as a collective entity, and also as a multiplicity of individual human beings, needs constantly to be adapting itself to its environment in order to survive (welfare) and grow (development). He lists certain states which describe man's relationship, biologically and sociologically, to his environment, under the four headings we have mentioned: welfare (to continue to function well) and development (to continue to advance); each with its respective opposite: ill-fare (failure to function well) and deterioration (failure to adapt). These are set out in Table 2. As Trist says: 'This whole set of terms therefore is concerned with the "dynamics" of adaptation' (Emery and Trist, 1975 edition, p. 126).

This approach to social systems can be used to describe features of the oscillation process in relation to religion. The adaptive features of social and political life occur at that mode which we call intra-dependence. We have already seen how religion is the institutionalisation of the transition between extra-dependence and intra-dependence. We suggest that religions can be classified as those which are functional, that is, they facilitate society's adaptive processes and hence encourage welfare and development; and those which are dysfunctional and lead to ill-fare and deterioration.

Let us examine this suggestion in more detail. According to the oscillation hypothesis, if society is to show signs of well-being and development, conditions need to be present which enable its members to make the transition from extra-dependence to intra-dependence and vice-versa. We have indicated that the states of mind of individuals who are entering the regression to dependence phase of the oscillation process display many of the characteristics listed by Trist under the heading of ill-fare, such as breakdown, vulnerability and dissociation. It is the experience of this condition which provides the dynamic for regression, in search of relief from the pain it causes.

We have proposed that human behaviour reflects two different kinds of mental activity: the activity which is dominant in intra-dependence is W-activity, whereas the dominant activity in extra-dependence is S-activity. During the regres-

Table 2. **Welfare and development, and their opposites (Trist)**

Welfare (Well-being)	Ill-fare (Ill-being)	Development (Progression)	Deterioration (Retrogression)
Intactness	Impairment	Maturation	Arrest
Robustness	Vulnerability	Learning	Retardation
Self-regulation	Breakdown	Extended adaptability	Restricted adaptability
Integration	Dissociation		
Independence[1]	Dependence[2]	Cultural accumulation	Stagnation
Interdependence[3]	Isolation		
Coordination	Scatter	Product accumulation	Waste
Cooperation	Conflict[4]		
		Environmental expansion	Contraction
		Innovation (Aggression)[5]	Obsolence (Passivity)[6]

[1] We would prefer 'autonomy'.
[2] In the sense of *eg* drug dependence.
[3] We would prefer 'mutual dependence'.
[4] Conflict here assumed as destructive. Conflict is also a necessary aspect of development (see [5]).
[5,6] Our additions to Trist's list.

sion phase S-activity becomes dominant as individuals seek to cope with their inner stress and anxiety. Our thesis is that the religion which provides the ritual setting in which fantasies, generated when S-activity is dominant, are transformed into resources which maintain the states of welfare and development when W-activity is dominant, can be called *functional religion*. An essential condition is that the ritual takes account of S-activity as natural without mistaking it for W-activity.

Functional religion

In functional religion we need to distinguish three steps in the ritual, if we are to understand the transition from the dominance of S-activity to the dominance of W-activity. The first ritual step is that which enables the individual to accept the naturalness of his feelings of pain and inner turmoil, and supplies him with symbols of a primal object, so that he can tolerate and learn to understand the internal chaos in which he views himself as a good object and a bad object simultaneously. The second ritual step allows for the potency of these fantasies (S-activity) and enables them to be expressed overtly in contemplation of the primal object, but at the same time provides opportunities for these fantasies to be tested against the realities of life. In other words, in a religious service the worshipper recognises that the words he is using and the feelings he is expressing are something to do with struggling after survival. At the same time he has sufficient sense of 'public' reality to be testing the symbolic action he is engaging in against his recalled experience of life. If he sings 'Onward Christian Soldiers', this does not stimulate him to take up arms against people with other beliefs. (If it does, we would say the religion of his congregation is no longer functional.) The ritual tries to maintain this tension, this struggling with the awareness of being in S-activity and at the same time of relating it to W-activity.

The third step is the ritualising of the transition from the dominance of S-activity to the dominance of W-activity. The ritual is designed to show how chaos and dark-foreboding – death – is replaced by peace and hope – life. It institutionalises regeneration, in which the sense of 'well-being' replaces the doom of 'ill-being'. The worshipper is given the opportunity, by participating in the symbolic action, to pass through the fantasies of death and destruction and cross the threshold into fantasies of wholeness, which now he can transform into the realities of living in the world. Receiving the elements at Holy Communion is possibly the most significant action symbolising the transition. It is W-activity deliberately treating fantasy as reality without confusing them. But if there is confusion at this point, there is a lapse into dysfunctional religion.

Here we have, of course, enunciated the 'ideal type' of functional religion. Even in the context of functional religion many individuals will have quite different experiences. We have suggested previously that this process may be largely at the unconscious level. People may engage in personal oscillation (see p. 54) without being aware of the pain and the chaos, without clearly differentiating S- and W- activities, and with no sense of transition or the resultant experience of stability and growth. Or on the other hand the worshipper may have contrasting experiences: not of regression, but of attraction; not of pain but of pleasure; not of impotence but of power; not of alienation from the primal object but of union with both God and fellow worshippers. The transitional phase is one of joy and love and hope. The issue is whether the elation is a flight from reality or an expression of that reality. It is possible to be so caught up in a corporate act that the individual loses his personal sense of boundary, so that the primal object on which there is regression is an idealised myth about the group, the perfect fellowship. There will also be times when, for example, the weekly cycle of oscillation recurs without the individual being conscious of his need to regress personally. The extra-dependent phase may then become more a celebration of past experience. This latter occurrence can obviously inter-act and inter-penetrate with our ideal type, but we would not wish to deviate from our hypothesis that religion is not functional unless the above three steps are followed through. This is true even if the final outcome is only built up over many oscillations as fragments and parts are gradually fitted together, possibly untidily, as the worshipper gropes his way to giving authentic expression of his freedom. But we need to turn to examine *dysfunctional religion* in order to put this statement into perspective.

Dysfunctional religion

As we have hinted, dysfunction can manifest itself at each or all of the three steps we have outlined for functional religion. At the first step there may be no effective means at hand to manage the pain and chaos; that is, to control the regression to extra-dependence. This causes the individual to regress into withdrawal (see p. 38f). In this condition he tries to opt out, to dull his pain, rather than to find support to tolerate it. Because of the urgent call to the routines of everyday life such a person will have to struggle back to the intra-dependent mode without the relief of renewal. Multiplied into the collective experience of the group, the group will ultimately display the characteristics of Trist's deterioration or retrogression, namely arrest, retardation, waste, contraction and obsolescence. Established religions in ancient cultures, such as the Old Coptic Church in Ethiopia, provide examples of this condition.

In the second step, the worshippers may be so caught up in their S-activity fantasies that they confuse them with reality. Here we use the plural 'worshippers' because it is more likely to occur collectively in the way that Bion describes, in which whole groups become overwhelmed with S-activity and behave accordingly. Undoubtedly some regression to extra-dependence is achieved but it is a defensive regression where things are exaggerated, taken to the extreme, become larger than life. The group's needs can never be wholly gratified, yet there are temporary states when the group is euphoric and all anxiety evaporates. Literalism takes over which can lead to behaviour which to the outsider is manifestly absurd, but the apparently serious worshippers can insist on the impossible; for example, that to have one's sins forgiven means to have them wiped out for ever and to become sinless; or that to have the Holy Spirit is to have power to do what Jesus did. Under this stimulus we can see how leaders of obscure sects can produce leaders who claim they are divine and who make unfulfillable promises to their followers. Such people soon become caught up in continual extra-dependence; any modest transition to intra-dependence would disillusion them. The only way out is to leave the faithful, or to be anathematized.

The problem of the third step is to find leadership which is sufficiently effective to control the energy activated by the fantasies of S-activity, and to mobilise this energy in W-activity. If such leadership (from themselves or others) is missing then worshippers can never work through their needs and anxieties to make an effective transition. They recognise the need to oscillate to intra-dependence but their heart will not be in it. They may passively accept the political and economic state of their society, and work diligently to earn their own living, but they do not fully engage with society at its depth because they cannot extricate themselves from a dependent frame of mind. The zeal of their activity around the house of worship may be taken as a sign of devotion by outsiders, but inwardly their transition to intra-dependence is never fully accomplished. Their religious standing, despite their verbal denials, remains suspect and they are caught up in the vicious circle of seeking absolution but never finding it. Hence they are caught up in the state of ill-being, which they may justify to themselves by becoming paranoid about the world in its sinfulness.

One common factor emerges clearly from this analysis of dysfunctional religion. In none of the instances we have mentioned has there been a proper transition to intra-dependence, to the phase of transformation. Consequently the society whose majority religions are dysfunctional will be unlikely to show many of the characteristics of the states of well-being and development.

But once again we have described an 'ideal type'. If all oscillation took place in the context of organised religion, (but it never will so long as human beings enjoy any freedom to think for themselves – a paradox here), then perhaps we would see a clearer split between functional and dysfunctional religion in practice. However the purpose of this section has been to indicate possible outcomes, and not prescribe them. Additionally, we cannot ignore personal oscillation, for example in private prayer and meditation. This can take several forms. It can signify an opting out of the corporate oscillation process because it is experienced as dysfunctional, though the person concerned still acknowledges the values and culture associated with the corporate religion. Secondly it can be a retreat for purposes of reinforcing the functional aspects of the corporate religion of which the individual is a part, a kind of booster. Thirdly it can indicate a complete rejection of the existing values of a society and the wish to alter the way the members of that society oscillate, as might be the case with a Marxist Christian. Fourthly it can be the action of a believer in another religious faith who carries on regardless of his immediate religious environment. This was the practice of some Christians under Roman persecution.

To this point we have utilised Trist's table to examine the activity associated with the extra-dependent mode. We now turn to explore some aspects of the alternate mode of intra-dependence.

The intradependent mode

If we assume the ideal type of intra-dependence, the states of welfare and development are both present interacting with each other. But though the respective terms incorporate their own values (*eg* learning is basic, innovation is desirable, co-operation is essential), in order to share the evolving social system, other values are also required. We have suggested that one of the conditions for functional religion is that the values attributed to the primal object in extra-dependence will pervade the social values of the environment. This presents us with two predicaments.

The first is that for social life to be just it must be adaptable to its environment, and as it does so some prevailing values will need to change. Thus the problem of controlling the birth-rate in an overpopulated country has changed the attitude towards contraception. But if a religion believes it has the truth, and its god is absolute, then its values will be fixed in the extra-dependent mode and may not be permitted to change in the intra-dependent mode. The second predicament is that we cannot be sure that the worshippers in extra-dependence have not attributed to their god the values they wish to preserve in daily life, so that they can be backed up by religious sanctions when they impose their values on others. This is the substance of Nietzsche's dismissal of Jews and Christians. Man has always been prone to make gods in his own image.

An issue raised by both predicaments is: since the regression phase is concerned with the inner world of the individual, how can corporate issues of society raised in intra-dependence be explored in extra-dependence? If the entire tribe or people is small enough to oscillate corporately – the 'long houses' of Borneo are a good example of a psychically-shared experience – then individualism is less of a problem, at least for the tribe. However, in countries like Britain there is a tendency for a person to lose his sense of corporateness under the stress of dealing with his own individual sense of chaos, a feature we have already noticed repeatedly in our conferences on human behaviour. Under these circumstances the values explored in extra-dependence are more likely to be concerned with individual survival than corporate health. When fantasies are tested against realities, the individual may only retain a limited awareness of the realities which are present in the intra-dependent mode. But this is where quality of leadership in extra-dependence is vital. Unless it can remain sensitive to the realities of society then its religion will become increasingly dysfunctional. Such leadership requires vigour and discipline of an intensity which may be beyond the capacity of worshippers whose job-interests are concentrated in the intra-dependent mode. They may be social reformers, skilled teachers or hard-headed businessmen, but in extra-dependence they can become surprisingly undiscriminating and accept values which they oppose when they are in intra-dependence. Because values do not exist apart from the people who embody them, only an individual prepared to sacrifice part of himself will subject his values to examination or be prepared to change them, because this entails readiness to cope with the uncertainty of its effects on himself in the future. The onus on truth and integrity becomes considerable, since his vested interests in both modes are challenged. He needs to be ready to receive new insights about his god, to admit his mistakes to his family and colleagues, and to be willing to change his attitudes to life generally.

Another issue common to the two predicaments is that values specify the quality of relationships, but do not necessarily specify who or what is to be related in this way. Thus different individuals or groups may regard love as a supreme value, but for one this means a caring relationship between the strong and the weak, for another it means a relationship between friends, and for another it means a sexual relationship. Similarly the word 'liberation' has political and spiritual meanings within the churches. When the churches in the Third World expected to see it manifested in political liberation, this raised suspicions in the minds of others for whom it meant spiritual liberation. In a unitary society there tends to be consensus about which relationships are expected to manifest which values. Those who lead worship need to anticipate the effects of social, political and religious pluralism upon values, and to set these ruthlessly before those who worship.

The predicaments remain. All we can do here is to offer explanations for behaviour and interpret experience. Functional religion can only be known by its fruits. We inherit values from worshippers of bygone days, which mirror the characteristics of the god they have worshipped. We can only make these values our own by being prepared to question whether they are authentic for our generation and to test them in the light of our experience. This presents a poser for Christians, who hitherto have taken for granted the idea of God as Father, but who are now accused of male chauvinism in rejecting the mothering of God. In societies where capitalism prevails, God is frequently treated as if he is a successful businessman, and the values of capitalism are not subject to genuine debate. Karl Marx's criticism of religion as 'the opiate of the people' is a criticism of dysfunctionalism in religion, which he considered led to uncritical acceptance of existing values and social structures. He maintained that the masses, chained and shackled in a society where elitist values were being reinforced by religion, were themselves helplessly turning to the same religious source for solace as a drug to dull the pain of their imprisonment.

Functional religion is open to judgment according to its capacity to offer a critique of the values of society. For its members to maintain the social states of welfare and development, certain conditions need to prevail, which include freedom, justice, creative energy, hope. These social conditions are constantly being eroded by people using power for their own ends, leading to dictatorship, oppression, conformity and despair. Nevertheless, if there are sufficient pockets of creative energy residual in a society characterised by ill-fare and deterioration, then revolutionary change is possible. But a revolution will only avoid further ill-fare if it is able to show that its revolutionary concept of society is capable of adaptation to the actual environmental conditions of the people.

The nature of functional religion becomes even more complex when one society contains many religious faiths, a condition which prevails today in many countries hitherto oriented towards Christianity, where the christian movement has provided symbols for the process. We have already argued that, through its regulation of the oscillation processes of society, religion can provide a bonding which enables a social grouping to be experienced as a social structure, rather than an aggregate of individuals, and that the character of the god or gods worshipped is reflected in the value-system of that society. This statement is generally true whether the religion is functional or dysfunctional. In the first centuries of the christian era emperor worship provided such bonding as there was, thus ensuring the *pax Romana*. Before Constantine adopted Christianity as his state religion in the early fourth century, its adherents were regarded as a sect whose symbolic action was sometimes disruptive of the State, and were 'rightly' called atheists. Except for its own membership gathered into the church, it did not synchronise the oscillation process for anyone.

We would maintain that for a society to be stable, and at the same time sufficiently adaptable to develop in accordance with the creative energies of its people, it requires a religious institution whose symbols are generally acknowledged throughout that society, even though not all members are necessarily attached to them to the same degree or interpret them in the same way. So if the dominant religion is functional, it can make it possible for that society to tolerate some dysfunctional religion, because there is always the hope that it will reform and become more functional.

Where religious symbols are not acknowledged widely, there is political and social instability. While for some this critical position has the attraction of being potentially open to new influences, it also provides great scope for opportunism. It can also create enormous stresses which may overwhelm the populace and lead to outbreaks of violence, which in turn result in the formation and growth of heavily defended sub-groupings, each with its own form of religion. To name but two countries, the Lebanon and Northern Ireland are tragic contemporary extreme examples, where the split is not actually caused by religious differences, but the sensitivity to differences in religious symbols provides a ready made arena for political conflict, which then aggravates the religious divergencies. In Northern Ireland it has at least forced the adherents of the different religious groups to consider the re-creation of symbolic activity in which groups hitherto mutually antagonistic can join.

Homo duplex

The view of human life which we have built up in the last two chapters is not new in its broad outline. In the fields of anthropology, sociology, political philosophy and psychology, many writers have over the years arrived at descriptions of social life, organisation and mentality which are not identical, but which have in common a binary rather than a unitary form, referred to by Durkheim as *homo duplex*. In Table 3 we have collected together some of the pairs of terms which have been employed.

While there is considerable variation in the precise connotation of these terms, those in the right-hand column, corresponding to extra-dependence, refer in general to conditions of identification and solidarity between the members of a group or community. Those in the left-hand column refer to conditions of differentiation, in which individuals take up different roles in the groups and institutions through which they secure a living and continue the struggle for life in the natural and social world.

Many of these writers also refer to a process of alternation between these two modes: we have already referred (p. 49) to Turner's model of society as a process of oscillation between structure and *communitas*.

We shall suggest that one of the indicators of functional religion is that it draws attention to, and reinforces, the binary structure of social life, whereas dysfunctional religion emphasises and builds up one mode, either extra-dependence or intra-dependence, and impoverishes the other. In the next chapter we shall analyse how this comes about.

Table 3. **Binary concepts of social life**

city of men	city of God	Augustine (426)
society	religion	Berger (1967)
small tranquility	great similarity	Confucius
grid	group	Douglas (1966)
science	ritual	Douglas (1966)
organic solidarity	mechanical solidarity	Durkheim (1893)
profane	sacred	Eliade (1959)
logical thought	pre-logical thought	Levy-Bruhl (1927)
contract society	status society	Maine (1888)
adaptation	identity	Mol (1976)
institution	grouping	Nadel (1951)
logical conduct	non-logical conduct	Pareto (1916)
oligarchic society	ideal republic	Plato
technological order	moral order	Radcliffe Brown (1952)
technical order	moral order	Redfield (1953)
Gesellschaft (Society)	Gemeinschaft (Community)	Tönnies (1887)
structure	communitas	Turner (1969)

Chapter 4

Process and Movement in Churches

In the first chapter we advanced the proposition that a congregation gathered for worship in a church may be seen as
manifesting a process and a movement. In the following two
chapters we described the process. We shall now place the
process in a specific context: that of life and worship in christian churches; or in other words in a context in which the
process is contained and clothed in the beliefs and symbols of
the particular movement originated by Jesus Christ. Our
main purpose is to delineate in more detail the forms taken by
functional and dysfunctional religion in a christian context.
We shall also begin to illustrate how the doctrines and rituals
of Christianity constitute vehicles or templates for the process.

Before we embark on this examination, let us take stock of
where we have arrived so far. We have endeavoured to analyse the process, using concepts derived from the human sciences, indicating how it underlies the way religion has
evolved in societies. We have suggested that what is manifest
in a society as religious behaviour is related to the experience
of the members of that society, as the tip of an iceberg is
related to its unseen bulk under water. We have also suggested that the influence of a religion in a society may be
regarded as functional or dysfunctional, according to
whether or not it fosters individual and communal welfare
and development.

We have thus provisionally accepted the proposition that
where symbolic action is a vehicle for the true expression of
our experience, it prepares and enables us to come to terms

with the realities of our world, physical and social. But does this actually happen in churches, or is it a deluding dream? As is well known, some critics of religion allege that, whatever the ostensible purpose of the churches may be, their effect is to divert the attention of their congregations from the realities of life in society. They argue that by directing people's attention to christian ideals and beliefs they provide them with a way of avoiding disturbing aspects of their own condition and of contemporary human experience. We shall examine these criticisms by considering the relationship between worship in church and everyday life, seeking to distinguish between patterns of religious behaviour which are a means of engaging with the realities of the worshippers' world, and those which provide a way of escape from them or justification for a simplistic view of them. Our object of study is thus religious behaviour, which we have already defined (p. 51) as:

> the behaviour of people, either individually or collectively, which represents (symbolically) dependence on some idea, thing or person, the implied nature or power of which is not wholly susceptible to rational explanation.

Religious behaviour and church life

The following analysis of religious behaviour is based primarily on a series of research projects, clergy seminars and conferences for church groups on various aspects of church life. The churches and participants involved were drawn mainly from the Church of England, but included members of the Free Churches and the Roman Catholic Church. We include under the heading 'church life' all the activities which members of a church would regard as expressions of what their church is and does. Asked to tell other members of a conference what their church is doing, groups have come up with long and detailed lists of organisations and activities, including liturgical services, evangelism, prayer groups, pastoral care and counselling by clergy and laity, christian education for all age-groups, inter-church activities, community service, church leadership and administration at local, district and national levels, fund-raising, and social and recreational activities. Lists have been longer and shorter than this, but all have included some corporate act of worship, either in a church building or in private homes. Our analysis focuses upon these acts of corporate worship, but assumes that any or all of the activities which make up 'church life' may have a function with respect to the process, whatever their manifest purpose.

We also assume that the life and activities of any church are inter-related as elements in a social system, which persists from week to week and year to year through performing some distinctive task in its locality. We examine the tasks of churches in a later chapter (see Chapter 7); it is sufficient to say here that the task of any church depends on factors such as the nature of the locality, the class and type of the population, the church tradition, the denomination, other churches in the locality, and the leadership style of the clergy and church council or equivalent body. Members of the congregation are generally unaware of this task, which must be distinguished from the activities of individuals and from their suppositions about the nature and purpose of the church. The analysis which follows is concerned primarily with the patterns of behaviour fostered by churches, and hence with their effect upon the life of their community, rather than with the behaviour of individuals. We are asserting that functional and dysfunctional religion are characterised by the types of individual behaviour described; we do not mean to imply that every individual in any church follows the same pattern.

An analysis of the oscillation pattern

The oscillation process may be represented schematically as in Diagram 1 (p. 73). The diagram represents the alternation, through time, of a typical individual within a worshipping group, between states of intra-dependence and extra-dependence. This is represented horizontally, in an attempt to avoid the emotional and theological associations of up and down. The process is continuous, but for the purposes of analysis we have distinguished between six periods in any one cycle, and their characteristic behaviour and frames of

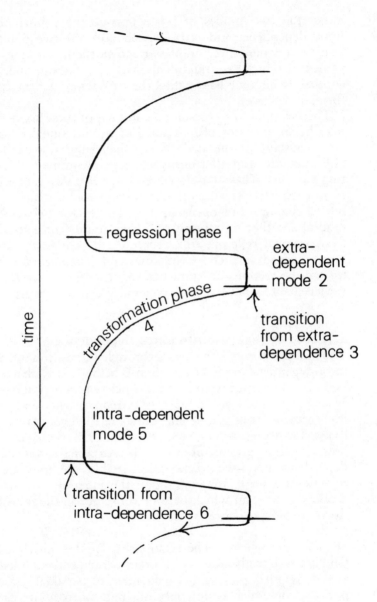

Diagram 1. **The oscillation process**
Numbers refer to the sections of chapter 4 which describe
these periods of the process.

mind: the two modes of relatedness to the primal object (intra-dependence and extra-dependence), the two points of transition when these modes are disturbed, and the two phases in which the individual changes from one mode to another, which we have called the regression and the transformation phases.

The behaviour of worshippers in each of these six periods may be an indicator of functional or dysfunctional religion. At each stage of the analysis we shall suggest what these indicators are, and offer terms to refer to a number of recurring patterns. These should be regarded as notes, rather than as an exhaustive treatment: each section could be developed into a chapter, and opens up possibilities for behavioural, biblical and theological research. Two important patterns of dysfunctional religion, folk religion and secularism, are in fact explored further in the following chapter. We have treated the sections on extra-dependence more briefly, since earlier chapters have already covered much of this ground.

1. Phase of regression to extra-dependence

The individual enters this phase through a transition from the intra-dependent mode (see section 6 below). It is characterised by the progressive dominance of S-activity over W-activity, and the transfer of attention and emotional involvement from people and things in the everyday world to psychic objects represented by symbols, in particular symbols of the 'primal object'. The experience of extra-dependence upon the primal object enables the individual to tolerate and begin to work upon the inner disorientation, weakness and pain which became conscious in the transition from intra-dependence.

a) Functional religion. The relationship of the individual to God is a responsible one. God is represented and experienced as just, requiring an acknowledgement of personal and corporate guilt which is not only felt but, since W-activity is subordinated but not suppressed, expressed in actual or intended restitution to other people. He is represented as a loving God who invites but does not impel the worshipper to come to him; and as a dependable God who can be relied upon by those who take up a dependent role. He is also represented as holy, so that the individual must acknowledge his alienation from God before he can approach him.

b) Dysfunctional religion. The individual blames his circumstances for his failures or distress, or attributes them to sickness or immaturity, or denies that they have any significance. He thus fails to own his feelings or past behaviour; he does not acknowledge guilt or shame, and the urge to seek for God is neutralised. He becomes passive, and W-activity becomes dissociated from S-activity. Consciously he looks for rational answers to his problems; unconsciously he enters a defensive regression, withdrawing into himself until the passage of time allows him to re-emerge into the world of practical affairs. This dysfunctional pattern may be termed *nominalism*. Insofar as an individual conforms to this pattern, he is unlikely to go to church very often, though he may rely on others to go to church on his behalf.

c) Movement and process. The character of the movement is crucial in this phase, since it supplies the symbols and rituals which the individual requires to make meaningful his feelings of fragmentation and his wish for a God on whom to depend. If the symbols of the movement do not give form to his experience in this way, because they are intrinsically inadequate or poorly presented, the individual cannot enter into a creative regression; he feels demeaned or let down, and resists becoming dependent.

In the 1662 Anglican service of Holy Communion, this phase is given liturgical form in the recitation of the Ten Commandments, the general confession, and the words of absolution by the priest, and in the self-examination, confession and restitution which are assumed to precede attendance at the service. In the Gospels, the distinction between dysfunctional and functional religion in this phase is perhaps best illustrated by Christ's vignette of the Pharisee and the publican who went up to the Temple to pray (Luke 18:9ff).

2. Mode of extra-dependence

In this mode the individual experiences relatedness to someone or something outside himself – a primal object – on whom he depends for life and well-being. His condition is not static: he may at different moments feel guilty, afraid, hopeful, joyful, grateful.

a) Functional religion. The individual engages in worship and contemplation of the glory, love and power of God, without altogether losing his sense of everyday reality. He continues to distinguish between symbolic objects and what they symbolise – between consuming the communion elements, for example, and receiving Christ. He is able to disagree with what is said and done in the service, without being put off or becoming contentious. In the terms employed earlier, S-activity is the dominant mode of thought, but W-activity is not suppressed or split off. The individual worships *with* other people, and *on behalf of* his family, community and nation, without becoming merged with any of these groups.

b) Dysfunctional religion. Perhaps the most familiar form is that in which W-activity is suppressed, and the individual loses his sense of distinctiveness from the worshipping group. He loses his capacity to distinguish between the symbol and the thing symbolised, and looks for immediate and magical answers to prayer. He may fear that small changes in the liturgy or in ritual acts will break the spell. This is the essence of *folk religion*; we return to it in more detail in Chapter 5 (see also Mensching, 1964). Insofar as the individual conforms to this pattern, he remains in a half-world between fantasy and reality; his regression to extra-dependence has been inadequately contained, and he is unprepared for the transition to intra-dependence.

In folk religion the gods worshipped may be clothed in the images of the movement, but someone who is not caught up in the process may perceive that they are embodiments of the needs and values of the local or national community which remain unmodified beneath their christian labels. The christian movement has been ineffective as a vehicle for regulating the regression to extra-dependence. At the other extreme, the symbols of the movement are accorded great reverence, but the same inability to distinguish between the symbol and the thing symbolised leads to fundamentalism, and to expectations that biblical and liturgical language, or the doctrine of the group leader, will literally describe what happens in the everyday world. This form may be termed *fanaticism*. It exercises powerful sanctions over its adherents' behaviour, who must give all their energy to its activities or become outcasts.

It will be seen that both these dysfunctional patterns are forms of idolatry.

Dietrich Bonhoeffer, writing about christian fellowship, draws a clear distinction between functional religion, which accepts the unhappy and ugly aspects of human relationships in the church, and fanaticism, which seeks to force conformity to an ideal:

> Innumerable times a whole Christian community has broken down because it had sprung from a wish dream (S-activity suppresses W-activity – *author's comment*). The serious Christian, set down for the first time in a Christian community, is likely to bring with him a definite idea of what Christian life together should be and try to realise it. But God's grace swiftly shatters such dreams. Just as surely as God desires to lead us to a knowledge of genuine Christian fellowship, so surely must we be overwhelmed by a great disillusionment with others, with Christians in general, and, if we are fortunate, with ourselves.
>
> ... God is not a God of the emotions but a God of truth. Only that fellowship which faces such disillusionment, with all its unhappy and ugly aspects, begins to be what it should be in God's sight, begins to grasp in faith the promise that is given to it ...
>
> ... The man who fashions a visionary ideal of community demands that it be realised by God, by others and by himself. He enters the community of Christians with his demands, sets up his own law, and judges the brethren and God Himself accordingly. He stands as a living reproach to all others in the circle of brethren ... When his ideal picture is destroyed, he sees the community going

to smash. So he becomes, first an accuser of his brethren, then an accuser of God, and finally the despairing accuser of himself. (Bonhoeffer, 1954 edition, pp. 16ff)

c) Movement and process. As we have indicated, the symbols supplied by the movement are put to various functional and dysfunctional uses by those engaged in the process.

Liturgical language is by definition the language of the extra-dependent mode, so that it is difficult to select examples. In the Holy Communion service the material most characteristic of *resting* in extra-dependence (as opposed to moving in and out of it) is that of the Sanctus, and, in the Anglican rites, of the preceding 'comfortable words'. It is expressive of the dynamic character of the liturgy (and reflected in the shape of the extra-dependent loop of the curve in Diagram 1) that this resting is not for very long: the service moves on to the communion itself and to the transition to intra-dependence.

In the New Testament the extra-dependent mode is clearly seen in the doctrinal sections of the letters of Paul and other writers (*eg* Romans 5–8; Ephesians 1–2; Hebrews 1–10:18). In these passages the writer expounds spiritual realities, with very few references to the circumstances of his readers or of himself.

3. Transition from extra-dependence

In this transition, through directing his attention to the primal object and expressing dependence upon it, the individual crosses a threshold between feeling separated from its power, goodness and wholeness (and therefore in himself weak, bad and fragmented), and feeling united with the object and possessing these qualities. The transition may only be noticed after it is past – as when one is rehearsing one's part in a play, and suddenly realises that one has *become* the character in the play, rather than merely simulating his behaviour. One sees the world of the play through the character's eyes. In worship the evidence that the transition has taken place is that the individual is increasingly oriented towards the day-to-day world, which he faces with power, wholeness and love. We have described the point of transition in a distinct section to emphasise that this is a 'flip-over' point which, as we shall see, may or may not take place.

a) Functional religion. Religion is not functional unless it supports a process in which this transition does take place. It takes place because the oscillation process is seen as a whole (cf. pp. 35ff on creative regression). Regression to extra-dependence is not a form of flight from the world, or an attempt to cling to childish dependence, but a means of engaging with its demands more resourcefully. God is seen as active both in the church and in the world; only the form of relatedness is different. *Laborare est orare*. It should be added that in functional religion the individual is united with the worshipping community as he is united with God through Christ.

b) Dysfunctional religion. The individual does not reach the point of transition to intra-dependence. He is therefore left without freedom or assurance of forgiveness, feeling weak and frightened in face of an omnipotent God whose goodness only reinforces his own guilt. He is unready to face the outside world, which takes on a menacing and unfriendly shape.

Those whose religion takes this form may return to their work and social life without in fantasy ever leaving the church. They may have to keep reassuring themselves by attending frequent week-day activities, under the guise of carrying out laudable spiritual, social and administrative responsibilities. This retarded state, which we refer to as *ecclesiasticism*, is thus a manifestation of insecure or resource-less dependence.

An alternative response to this failure to make the transition to intradependence is to blame and reject the liturgy and rituals of the church and lead a breakaway search for better ones. Insofar as this is a defensive device, used to deny resistance within the breakaway group to acknowledging guilt and regressing to extra-dependence, and attributing all the inadequacy to the liturgy, it leads to another dysfunctional form which we have called *sectarianism*. In sectarianism the failed transition from extra-dependence leads to fight and flight (see Appendix for a description of the fight-flight pattern of behaviour); in ecclesiasticism it leads to reinforced dependence.

c) Movement and process. In the Holy Communion service, this transition is given ritual expression in the eating and drinking of the consecrated elements. Up to this point Christ has been addressed and contemplated as an external figure. Now he is symbolically internalised, not as an alien presence but as the ordinary food which supports human life; as we shall see in the next section, he is not received in order to dominate from within (which is a form of extra-dependence), but is 'digested' into the personality ('Feed on him in thy heart ...').

The New Testament depicts a clear distinction between the behaviour of the disciples before and after this transition. When they depend upon him as a person separate from themselves they are weak, fearful and uncomprehending. When he is 'in' them, and they are 'in' him, after the coming of the Holy Spirit, they speak and act with power, courage and insight. The Holy Spirit might perhaps be regarded as God as he is known in intra-dependence; 'He is the Spirit that makes us sons (intra-dependence), instead of slaves (extra-dependence)' (Romans 8:15).

The following account, by a member of a working group who were closely involved in the development of these ideas, illustrates how an individual recognised and began to resist what appears to be a tendency to ecclesiasticism in his church. (The references to the Kingdom of God in this and later illustrations will be more fully explained in Chapter 6):

The church is an active one, and has a range of activities taking place practically every evening of the week, not to mention lunch clubs every week day. At the main Sunday services, after the service proper, but before the dismissal, a period of time is given over to notices. Various members of the congregation get up and announce forthcoming events or projects, often asking for volunteers to help out. Although people usually make themselves known to the various organisers at coffee after the service, occasionally they are requested to identify themselves in this part of the service itself.

I have attended the church irregularly for about five years. Irregularly, because of being away for weekends, but also of late because of some feeling of guilt at being unable – and unwilling – to participate in the activities, many of which are very commendable, but with which I just do not want to get involved during the week. I have my own life to lead, quite a lot of work to do in the evenings, and a circle of friends, some of whom have nothing at all to do with any church. In many cases I prefer their company to that of fellow members of the congregation of the church. And since the church serves a special-ised community, I do not wish to get involved with them. Nonetheless I felt guilty about not participating. I felt myself not to be pulling my weight, to be taking out of the church but putting nothing in. The dismissal at the end of the service sounded manipulative. I was not sure I could 'go forth in peace' feeling as I did that I was failing the institution.

As I began to gain some insight into the significance of the oscillation process, I began to find a new sense of free-dom about going to church. For years I had believed that all areas of my life were part of my service of God, but (as I now realise on looking back) my guilt about not wanting to be involved in church activities had eroded my sense of the value of my other activities. An appreciation of the meaning of the Kingdom of God enabled me to give value to what I was already doing so that I was free to bring these concerns into my worship instead of being preoc-cupied with other concerns which I felt I ought to have. I can go out from church feeling what I am doing is impor-tant rather than guilty for not supporting the church's activities.

4. Phase of transformation to intra-dependence

This phase is represented in Diagram 1 as a shallow curve, to indicate that the 'digestive' process, by which the charac-teristics of the primal object are internalised, W-activity becomes dominant again and S-activity is subordinated, takes place over an extended period. The individual is faced with the realities of life in his family, in his neighbourhood, in his place of work, and in his nation and in the world as a whole, and he now sees them in the light of his experience of worship. To the extent that the constructs which shape his experience have been sharpened and changed by the experience of worship, he finds his world different. This may be exciting, threatening or saddening. It may demand changes in attitude and behaviour. All this takes time.

Characteristically this phase entails mourning. The clarity and wholeness of moments of vision are lost; the incompleteness of the response to the primal object becomes more evident; the intractable otherness of the material and social world outside the church re-asserts itself. As Dahrendorf (1974) said of an analogous transition in his Reith lectures:

> ... As we move from the world of goals and purposes to the world of action, the imperfections of men become as painfully evident as the obstreperousness of existing things.

a) Functional religion. The individual recognises that he confronts the possibilities and problems of existence as a human being among other human beings. He knows his own autonomy, and accepts that he is responsible for making judgments according to his perception of the world around him. He also recognises that his judgments are affected by the values he has attributed to the God he worshipped in church. In devotional terms, the constructions which he places upon the situations he enters – which are *his* constructions – have been moulded by the constructs of justice and injustice, freedom and bondage, love and rejection, good and evil, which were implicit and explicit in the liturgy. As he arrives at this recognition and acts upon it, the individual changes his role from that of worshipper to those appropriate to the various groups and institutions he enters as a human being. He does not see the church as having a monopoly over human existence, but by his behaviour asserts that God has. He remains in a condition of dependence, but of a different kind from that which he experienced during the act of worship. There his dependence was clearly on God beyond himself, transcendent. Now his behaviour reflects God within himself, immanent, and yet the more firm is this inward dependence, the more liberty he has to think and act as a responsible person.

Marion Milner (1956) has described this transformation to intra-dependence in her interpretation of William Blake's sequence of paintings illustrating the book of Job. Of one of the later pictures in the sequence she writes:

> It seems that Job no longer needs the omnipotent Father God commanding from above-within and identified with the 'wrought image' of himself, for he has found a kind of control that is inherent, part of what is controlled, not separated and split off. He has found a power that transcends the duality of controller and controlled. 'And that day ye shall know that I am in my Father and you in me and I in you' says the text. Thus the psyche is surely no longer split into a part which orders and a part which obeys – or rebels. The resulting control of instinct is based on love rather than fear.

This transformation is obstructed to the extent that the individual is unable to let go and mourn the fantasies of omnipotence which arise in the extra-dependent state. He is tempted to think that he is perfect, that he can work miracles, that God will rig events in his favour, that he will never die. To the extent that these fantasies persist as determinants of his everyday behaviour, he conforms to patterns of dysfunctional religion.

b) Dysfunctional religion. There is little or no capacity for change, because the incompleteness of the oscillation process has meant that there is little to transform. There is disappointment, because the individual had hoped to change and in fact feels impotent, but nothing to mourn. Life has a sameness modified only by the wrinkling of age and by the need to react to external circumstances. This phase exposes the poverty of nominalism and folk religion, and forces those caught up in ecclesiasticism and sectarianism to greater exertions, because they do not recognise why they are inwardly unable to change. Without this insight they blame the world for not changing, because it is generally unimpressed and resistant to their exhortations. Ecclesiasticism and sectarianism compensate for their inadequacy in regulating the oscillation process by carrying religion into secular life. People are required to feel extra-dependent, when the demands of their working and social life are that they take responsibility for their actions and behave autonomously. This activity is often mistakenly called mission or evangelism. In its extreme form it is more accurately defined as *proselytism*, which can be seen as the activity of those who seek justification for their own stance – a justification they do not find in themselves – by persuading and manipulating others to become like themselves. Proselytism leads not to the liberty of intra-dependence, but to domination by a primal object who commands, in Marion Milner's terms, from 'above-within'.

c) Movement and process. The concluding section of the 1662 Communion Service, following the reception of the elements, is brief, and turns the attention of the worshipper to the life he or she will lead on leaving the place of worship. In the modern revisions of this liturgy this section is even briefer, thrusting the worshipper summarily into the world. In view of the dynamics of the oscillation process as we have analysed it, the Gloria seems to be more satisfactorily placed before the communion rather than after it, where it invites regression back to extra-dependence: ' ... Thou that sittest upon the right hand of God the Father, have mercy upon us'. At this stage in the service the flow of the process requires that the congregation should, in terms of an episode in the Gospels beloved by preachers, leave the mountain of Transfiguration and return to the ugly realities of the valley.

This phase is represented in the New Testament letters by the concluding sections setting out the implications of the Gospel for parents, children, rulers and citizens (*eg* Romans 12–15; Colossians 3–4; 1 Peter 2:11–4:19; Hebrews 13). In a later chapter (Chapter 6) we shall suggest that the Kingdom of God, as delineated by Christ, stands for the life of society in the intra-dependent mode. In this phase the role of the individual as church member therefore becomes dormant, as he takes up roles in the unseen realm of God.

5. Mode of intra-dependence

Whereas the activities characteristic of the extra-dependent mode can be summed up in the word 'worship', the activities of the intra-dependent mode are many and various, since they comprise all those activities in which the individual seeks to understand, master and respond to his physical and social world. He recognises that this world is not under his magical control and does not owe him a living. He confronts it as one whose survival, well-being and development are in his own hands, in that he has no magical protection; yet also outside his control, in that he is a vulnerable creature, subject to accident, disease, violence, ageing and death. W-activity is thus dominant; yet S-activity is not suppressed. The individual displays in his behaviour the values he contemplated in the extra-dependent mode. He invests his own life, and that of society, with meaning; he thinks and acts as one who is related to the physical world and to other people. He is able to tolerate the anxieties of dependence on others, and work constructively with it, because he has internalised the idea of a benign and creative dependent relationship.

a) Functional religion. Functional religion is known in this mode by its invisibility. If the transition from extra-dependence and the ensuing transformation phase have been functional, the individual is free to take up the roles required of him by the demands of living: to earn a living, the role of worker; to raise a family, the role of parent; to help someone, the role of neighbour. These are only classes of roles: the worker may for example be a welder, mechanic, nurse, policeman, accountant, housewife, artist, teacher, shop-keeper, social worker, chef or politician. Overlapping with these roles is that of citizen, which may lead him in many directions in seeking to love his neighbour – party member, voter, councillor, statesman, agitator and revolutionary.

In his roles in society he is on a par with those around him engaged in the same tasks. His christian resources are interior and personal to himself, to be offered in the pursuit of the common goal. To the extent that he insists on a religious, christian or God label he has not made the transition to the intra-dependent mode, and his autonomy is illusory.

c) Dysfunctional religion. Dysfunctional religion is not invisible: it wants to be noticed through the attention it pays to the affairs of men in the name of God. We shall describe two types.

The first type arises from the attempt, by the State, to impose unity on diversity, and hence we have adopted for it a term also used by others (*eg* Bellah, in Richey and Jones (eds) 1974, p. 21 and *passim*): *civil religion*. It appears in two forms: one in which the State officially promotes a religion to gain power and credibility or to unite a shaky empire; the other in which a religion evolves to protect the integrity of the State in the eyes of its citizens.

The former is exemplified by Constantine's adoption in AD 320 of an already existing minority religious system, Christianity, to hold together the Roman empire. The symbols of Christianity were invested with political significance, Constantine had them incorporated into his royal standards, and Roman emperors set the precedent for being installed into office with christian ceremonies. The church, as the guardian of this religion, was expected to reinforce the values of the State, and some uniformity of religious practice was essential since it was vital to the emperor's survival – a policy backed up with dungeon, fire and sword.

With the expansion of European culture and the development of world trade, sovereigns had progressively to concede more freedom to their subjects, and submit to the modification of this uniformity. As this relaxed approach was succeeded by pluralism in religious behaviour the second form of civil religion emerged. In its original form civil religion was an instrument of politics: the conflict between Beckett and Henry II in 1170 was over this issue. In its later form, the State can only look to religion to give some credibility to its policies. For instance when in a democratic country citizens are responsible for electing their government, the traditional religious institutions may carry on as before, but they may lose support from their members if they challenge the State which these members have instituted in their roles as citizens. If they are afraid of this confrontation, religious leaders find they are not in a position to subject their own human values to critical examination, and submit to the status quo. Likewise citizens shop around for religious gatherings which reflect their own personal beliefs and prejudices and do not raise awkward questions about them. Thus civil religion appears to be benign, but in fact it leads to the erosion of functional religion, since the civic values of the intra-dependent mode invade the rituals of the extra-dependent mode and pose critical questions for those seeking to observe functional religious practices, who are seen as a disaffected minority.

The second type of dysfunctional religion in the intra-dependent mode may in part be one of the consequences of civil religion. Advocates of this religious type are sensitive to the ill-effects of nominalism, folk religion, ecclesiasticism, sectarianism and proselytism, which they see to be sources of injustice, waste, stagnation and the other factors listed by Trist as indicators of ill-fare and deterioration in social systems. They tend to see gatherings of Christians for worship as self-indulgent, unless they lead directly to social action to correct the inequalities of society. Human need is defined in this way, with the result that religious values are reinterpreted in secular terms. Speaking technically, they demythologise the teaching of Jesus, so that injunctions which at face value relate to God and the supernatural are applied concretely to mankind in the here and now, to such an extent that the first and great commandment becomes to love your neighbour, demoting the love of God to second place. This is *secularism*.

A point to notice is the similarity of secularism to much of what we have depicted as functional religion in intra-dependence. Both are active in the service of mankind; both display a deep concern for those who are deprived by mismanagement or biased government; both seek to identify themselves closely with those whom they serve; and both see the incarnation of Jesus as a model for their behaviour. But whereas functional religion derives its power and insight from extra-dependence, most of the adherents of secularism would argue that worship which stresses dependence upon God leads to childish and unsophisticated behaviour which is inadequate, inappropriate and even damaging because of its assumptions about the nature of man. As well as reacting in this way against folk religion, secularists frequently make the assumption that God is in all men by virtue of their birth, and that inter-dependence and brotherly love are attitudes in which the 'worthship' of God (the original Anglo-Saxon form of worship) is more fully realised, in that they lead to more worthy contributions towards an ideal society than prayers to God that his Kingdom will come. For secularism, intra-dependence is not merely one of two alternating modes of human consciousness, but the normative and only constructive one.

In each of these dysfunctional types of religion there is a confusion of function between the State and religious institutions. In civil religion the State takes over the churches. In secularism churches take over the task of the State, instead of preparing worshippers to take up their roles as citizens. There is another similarity, in that both are élitist religious forms, for rulers or intelligentsia, which tend to consign the populace to other forms of dysfunctional religion and their consequences, folk religion being the most likely.

c) Movement and process. As we have indicated, the Bible and the liturgy have a theology of the intra-dependent mode, but this theology is not explicit in the activities of this mode. Overt use of the language and rituals of the extra-dependent mode in everyday affairs is generally an indicator of dysfunctional religion. This section is therefore necessarily brief.

Establishing the distinctiveness of the two modes in his own life brings the individual both release and loneliness. This is illustrated by the following account:

> In my previous home my involvement with the local church in a deprived inner-city area seemed to burn up every waking moment, with youth club work, Bible Class, summer playschemes, Deacons' Meetings and ten-

ants' campaigns. After five years it was eating up so much of my life I felt I had to leave the area to recover any existence of my own.

I swung to the opposite end of the pendulum, finding it increasingly difficult to find any meaning or satisfaction in church worship. I struggled to forge some kind of live connection between my growing political consciousness and activity and my christian commitment, but the struggle was a bleak one. The culture and the assumptions behind the worship seemed in complete contradiction to my experience of life in the inner city. While my daily experience as a community worker made me aware of the deep and evil injustices and conflicts of interest between groups and classes of people, church services seemed to assert a blander, cleaner view of society in which problems could be 'reconciled' at the level of personal relationships. They seemed to be preaching 'Peace, peace' when there was no peace. On two occasions the revulsion I felt was so great that I walked out of the service, fuming with anger and revulsion.

The concept of the oscillation process, and the insight it gave me into the distinction between the Church and the Kingdom of God, came as a way out of the trap: oscillation, not incorporation. The Church is not the Kingdom of God, but the door into it. There was no need to incorporate all my political activity and community action into the church, and in fact it was quite inappropriate to do so. This was liberation. I could trust that my working concerns with social justice, righteousness and peace were part of my membership of the Kingdom of God. I felt free to join with others, many of them not Christians, engaged in the same struggles to work out what justice meant in practice in concrete situations, without feeling a need to bring the church as an institution into these struggles or to take them back into the church for incorporation into its life.

This insight released me to start going to church again, to acknowledge my dependence and find personal refreshment. At times in services great waves of emotion swept over me, as though a backlog of dependence which had been able to find no acknowledgement or outlet in years of community and political activity found expression. (It is now) possible for me to worship with those whose political views I passionately oppose, and to join in political activity with other socialists, without feeling under impossible pressure to harmonise all aspects of life in a consistent religious stance. I can hold a socialist analysis of society, defining the fundamental issues in terms of class conflict, and a christian analysis which defines the one thing people have in common beyond class divisions, a common status as sons of God.

In practice I still find it difficult to hold on to these two stances. I am acutely conscious that the church to which I turn for worship is itself as an institution part of the established structure of power and privilege I am opposing politically on many issues (*eg* church investments in property and in South Africa). Equally difficult is the fact that many of the political groups I work with see religious belief as a distortion of the truth and a hindrance to social progress. (This) insight about oscillation helps me not to deny the contradictions, but to act as a representative of my political commitments within the church and the christian faith within political groups.

6. Transition from intra-dependence

In intra-dependence the individual takes for granted the aims and values which he brings to his various activities, and engages in them with energy and confidence. He tolerates the uncertainties and ambiguities of the world he faces, and the anxieties which accompany the satisfactions of responding to it. In colloquial terms, he feels good about it.

The transition to extra-dependence takes place when these values can no longer be taken for granted, and these uncertainties and anxieties cease to be tolerable. The individual's attention shifts from the realities of his world to his own feelings of self-doubt, confusion, fatigue, guilt and weakness. He is beginning to feel bad about it. The transition from extra-dependence was an integrative process, towards wholeness. The transition to extra-dependence is a process of fragmentation, in which W-activity is subordinated to S-activity.

The transition may take place because the individual has been stretched beyond his limits by the demands of life. It may take place when these demands are not great, but the limitations of the individual's system of values are such that they can be sustained no longer. It may take place when the individual is relatively untroubled, but seeks the re-creation of an opportunity to regress to dependence. It may take place at times and places which have become habitually established as part of the rhythm of his life, such as Sunday worship or annual festivals.

a) Functional religion. On all these occasions the transition demands a willingness and capacity to let go of autonomy and allow feelings and fantasies of chaos and helplessness to come into consciousness. The individual takes the brakes off S-activity and releases himself into extra-dependence. He views his recent actions, not with the calculated judgments of W-activity, but as manifestations of his relatedness to God, and to other people and to the created order. His failures are experienced as sin against God and man, and he acknowledges his share in the corporate responsibility of the sin of mankind.

The transition also requires belief in someone or something outside himself which will support him as he regresses to dependence. The way this belief is put into words is not in itself important: what is essential is that some such belief has been built up through past experience of depending on others. If past experience has not given rise to this belief ... but to pursue this would lead us into the consideration of dysfunctional transitions. In a christian context this belief is given substance through the vehicles of the movement, such as the Bible, the liturgy, and pastoral teaching, which enrich and mould his images of a primal object. He can believe that if he turns to God he will be in good hands, even though for some it may be 'a fearful thing to fall into the hands of the living God' (Hebrews 10:31).

The individual takes the risk of trusting that, if he regresses to extra-dependence, he will not fall out of those hands. He accepts the fantasy role of a little child before a heavenly Father, even if, rightly or wrongly, he imagines that this will shake the belief of his business colleagues or of members of his family in his sophistication and maturity. In biblical terms, he accepts the stipulation of Jesus that 'unless you turn and become like children you will never enter the kingdom of heaven' (Matthew 18:3).

b) Dysfunctional religion. Failure to make an effective transition from intra-dependence can be detected as the origin of several forms of dysfunctional religion. *Nominalism* originates in the individual's incapacity to become like a child – to allow S-activity to become dominant and to imagine himself in the presence of God. This incapacity may be culturally determined as well as personally willed. All the individual can and will do is to seek rationalistic answers to his problems: W-activity becomes dissociated from S-activity, and in the latter mode he uses regression as a defence against facing unresolved issues in his inner world – the strategy we have referred to as withdrawal (cf p. 39). From this withdrawal he emerges unchanged.

Folk religion is an expression of the desire to flee from the harsh realities of the world of intra-dependence. The individual allows himself to be absorbed in a worshipping group in which S-activity has suppressed W-activity. In this defensive regression the individual is filled with grotesque and seductive images which evoke nameless fears and entice with magical powers. Out of such stuff is the primal object fashioned.

Secularism can be traced to a wish to avoid the dysfunctional aspects of folk religion by avoiding regression to extra-dependence altogether. To the secularist extra-dependence is a demonstration of weakness in an adult, and manifestations of S-activity are seen as a form of sickness. The attempt is therefore made to construct a religion from a non-dependent interpretation of christian values. The attempt is unsuccessful, in that the secularist is dissociated into two parts, the conscious rational part pursuing the secularist programme, while the unconscious irrational part regresses into the extra-dependent mode. Seeking to save his life in W-activity, he loses it in S-activity. We consider secularism in more detail in the next chapter.

Another religious type, the *cult*, which we have not mentioned hitherto, may be traced to this point in the cycle. Briefly, the cults may be characterised as attempts to refine the grotesque and seductive images which arise in the transition to extra-dependence, and to employ them as secret guides to the supernatural. The mood is one of expectancy (see Appendix for an account of this culture). The devotee hopes through liaison with these 'powers' and 'spirits' to obtain guidance and knowledge of events outside human competence. The dependence is upon that which is about to be revealed; characteristically, in this culture, that which *is* revealed never satisfies. The devotee therefore tends to move from one cult – spiritism, astrology, witchcraft – to another, always seeking a god but paradoxically always running away from the God who would cause him to see through his veil of illusion.

c) Movement and process. As we have tried to show, transitions to extra-dependence are inevitable, sooner or later. All that is in question is whether they contribute to a creative process, in which W- and S-activity are integrated, or whether the process is defensive, with W- and S-activity dissociated from one another. The movement gives form to the primal object evoked in extra-dependence, and facilitates a creative regression.

The christian movement calls the individual to repent and believe the Gospel, through the evangelist (see Chapter 8), and liturgically in the injunction to confession and the offer of forgiveness. Only too often, unfortunately, the evangelist's call has been delivered in such crude terms that the individual's anxiety about the consequences of regression to extra-dependence has turned to rage against the symbols he has been offered. This has led to resistance to acknowledging the emotional realities of the process, which the language of the movement interprets in theological terms.

This analysis may be summarised as in Table 4 p. 94. What we have referred to as functional religion we now propose to call *apostolic religion*, in the context of the christian

Table 4.

Stage in Oscillation Process	Functional	Key stages for different dysfunctional patterns of behaviour (Types of Religion)							
Regression to E/D	Apostolic	Nominalism							
E/D mode	"		Folk religion	Fanaticism					
Transition from E/D	"				Ecclesiasticism	Sectarianism			
Transformation to I/D	"						Proselytism		
I/D mode	"	Nominalism	Folk religion					Civil religion	Secularism
Transition from I/D	"									Cults

E/D = extra-dependence　　　I/D = intra-dependence

movement. As we have noted there are other historical movements, and at this point we do not wish to make judgments about their functional and dysfunctional possibilities.

Throughout this analysis we have written in a way which may seem to depict a world in which every act of worship is, for some, a crisis, akin to conversion, and in which the distinction between functional and dysfunctional religion is very sharply drawn. It should be made clear that what we have described are 'ideal types'; that is, contrasting models depicted in such a way as to alert the reader to features of behaviour in the much more varied and ambiguous situations of 'real' life.

It should also be stated that, while we have expressed critical judgments about many forms of religious behaviour, which we regard as dysfunctional, we are not implying that the individuals who practise these religious forms are dishonest or lack integrity. We are however asserting that those who become caught up in the patterns of collective worship we have described become part of a process which is likely to be dysfunctional for themselves and for their society.

Concluding illustration

Having pointed out the ways in which accounts of individual religious behaviour can be misleading, we would like to conclude this chapter with an illustration from literature, which takes an autobiographical form, but which crystallises many elements in the oscillation process as we have described it.

Tolstoy's uncompleted short story, *The Memoirs of a Madman*, which was never published in his life-time, describes a prolonged crisis in the life of the narrator, and is clearly in part autobiographical. The title of the story may be ironical: the events of the story depict a man coming to his senses. The crisis begins when the man is thirty-five: so Tolstoy is describing what would now be called a mid-life crisis!

Up to this point the narrator has lived an unexceptional life:

Like all mentally healthy boys of our circle I entered the high school and afterwards the university, where I completed the course of law-studies. Then I was in the Civil Service for a short time, and then I met my present wife, married, had a post in the country and, as it is called, 'brought up' our children, managed the estates, and was Justice of the Peace (1935 edition p. 213).

There are earlier references to his interest in childhood in the story of the crucifixion, but none in the account of his adult life. It would be compatible with the narrative to describe his pattern of religious behaviour during this period as one of nominalism.

The narrator's first attack occurs when he is travelling to another province to buy an estate. In the coach he awakes from sleep feeling unaccountably afraid and imagines he might die on the journey. They stop at an inn which he says 'appeared terribly melancholy to me, so much that it seemed uncanny and I got out of the coach slowly' (p. 215). Fantasy is taking hold of him: we may see this as the beginnings of a transition from intra-dependence.

He sleeps in the inn and wakes up in terror. His sense of the meaning and purpose of his journey and of his life have deserted him. He reflects:

Why have I come here? Where am I betaking myself? Why and whither am I escaping? I am running away from something dreadful and I cannot escape it ... It is myself I am weary of and find intolerable and a torment ... I cannot get away from myself ' ... 'But what folly is this!' I said to myself. 'Why am I depressed? What am I afraid of?' 'Me!' answered the voice of Death, inaudibly. 'I am here!' (p. 216).

Tolstoy describes his state of mind vividly and at length. Eventually his thoughts turn to God. The christian movement which is part of his culture provides him with a vehicle through which regression to extra-dependence is possible. But his nominal adherence to his religion becomes manifest: he is unable to regress:

For some twenty years I had not prayed, and I did not believe in anything, though as a matter or propriety I fasted and went to communion every year. Now I began to pray. 'Lord, have mercy!' 'Our Father.' 'Holy Virgin.' I began to compose new prayers, crossing myself, bowing down to the ground and glancing around for fear that I might be seen. This seemed to divert me – the fear of being seen distracted my terror – and I lay down. But I had only to lie down and close my eyes for the same feeling of terror to knock and rouse me ... (p. 217).

He returns from his journey and continues his life superficially as before. But he is terrified of falling prey to his depression, and has 'to live without stopping to think, and above all to live in my accustomed surroundings'. As a defence against facing the terrors aroused in him by the unfamiliar, he falls into the pattern we have called ecclesiasticism when it is characteristic of a church:

... I continued to live as before, only with this difference, that I began to pray and went to church ... Everything seemed dull to me and I became pious (p. 218f).

He has to make a trip to Moscow, and in his hotel the horror returns. Life has no purpose, yet he is afraid to kill himself. Yet if he goes on living he does so only in order to die. He prays again, and this time his prayers have meaning. He demands an answer to his questions and there is no reply. He becomes indignant:

I did not believe in him, but I asked, and He did not reveal anything to me. I was balancing accounts with Him and blaming Him. I simply did not believe (p. 222).

Although the word is not used, Tolstoy seems to depict the narrator's state following this episode as one of despair. Ecclesiasticism has proved an ineffective defence against his loss of meaning. He is in a state of relative extra-dependence, in which he feels alienated from God, unable to make contact with him and so make the transition to intra-dependence:

I went to church on Sundays and feast days, prepared to receive Communion, and even fasted ... I did not expect any result from this, but as it were kept the demand-note and presented it at the due date, though I knew it was impossible to secure payment ... I did not fill my life by estate management ... but by reading magazines, newspapers and novels, and playing cards for small stakes (p. 222).

In the terms used by Alcoholics Anonymous, he has 'hit bottom'. He has no further defence against the knowledge of his incapacity to confer meaning on his own life. Out of this formlessness either something new will emerge, or he will spend his time in futile activity, waiting to die – the condition described earlier in section 4 as that resulting from the failure to make the transition to intra-dependence.

He goes out hunting on foot, becomes separated from his companions, and thinks himself lost in the forest. He is seized with terror, but this time his response is different:

My heart palpitated, my arms and legs trembled. 'Is this death? I won't have it! Why death? What is death?' Once again I wanted to question and reproach God, but here I suddenly felt that I dare not and must not do so, that it is impossible to present one's account to God, that He had said what is needful and I alone was to blame. I began to implore his forgiveness, and felt disgusted with myself.

The horror did not last long. I stood there for a while, came to myself, went on in one direction and soon emerged from the forest. I had not been far from its edge, and came out on the road. My arms and legs still trembled and my heart was beating, but I felt happy. I found the hunting party and we went home. I was cheerful, but I knew there was something joyful which I would make out when alone. And so it was. I remained by myself in my study and began to pray, asking forgiveness and remembering my sins. There seemed to me to be but few, but when I recalled them they became hateful to me (p. 224).

The expression 'I ... came to myself ' might be taken as a

colloquial way of referring to the integration of W- and S-activity in the transformation in intra-dependence. His restored reality-sense is seen in his finding his way out of the forest, and in his clear distinction between the insignificance of his sins as regards their impact on the world, and their hatefulness to him as he contemplates them in the presence of God.

The denouement of the story as we have it occurs shortly afterwards. He describes it as the beginning of his madness. He goes to church and receives Communion, and notices beggars at the door:

> And it suddenly became clear to me that this ought not to be, and not only ought not to be but in reality was not. And if this was not, then neither was there either death nor fear, and there was no longer the former tearing asunder within me and I no longer feared anything.
>
> Then the light fully illumined me and I became what I am now. If there is nothing of all that – then it certainly does not exist in me. And there at the church door I gave away to the beggars all I had with me – some thirty-five roubles – and went home on foot talking with the peasants (p. 225).

For the purposes of this study this conclusion has a nice ambiguity. Our first response may be to regard this as a manifestation of functional apostolic religion. Tolstoy appears to regard it as such – yet the title of the story, and hints in the introductory paragraphs, suggest that he may perceive a manic quality in the narrator's statements. Is this functional intra-dependence or fanaticism, which we have described as characterised by an 'inability to distinguish between the symbol and the thing symbolised . . . and expectations that biblical and liturgical language . . . will literally describe what happens in the world' (p. 77)? We have defined functional religion as that which fosters welfare and development in a society. In the feudal society of Tolstoy's time, what kind of behaviour would make more than a fleeting impact on the 'ill-fare' of the peasants, and promote the development of the whole society? Tolstoy did not live to see how this question was decisively answered.

This ambiguity in the significance of our illustration may remind us that the terms we have proposed are tools for raising questions about the expectable outcome of different patterns of worship in a community, rather than labels assigning fixed positive and negative values to them.

Chapter 5

Folk Religion, Secularism and Apostolic Religion

At the risk of some repetition we wish to examine the impli-
cation of the above analysis for what we consider to be major
types of religion in western industrial society. In societies
with other basic religious movements their manifestation will
take on different shapes, but the underlying principles remain
the same.

Folk Religion
   Earlier (p. 76) we described folk religion as arising where
individuals seek some symbolic action and language to
embody myths which have been transmitted from person to
person in ways which elude description. Carl Jung's concept
of the collective unconscious (Jung, 1940, 1959) is one explanation of the persistence of myths of heroes, saviours, magi-
cians and great mothers. Within the limitations imposed by
this study it is sufficient to point out that the myths projected
from the unconscious need symbolic expression and hence
lead to the development of sacred symbols. In primitive
tribes these sacred symbols are products of the natural environment, such as sacred trees, stones, and hills. Under the
dominance of a movement which introduces its own symbols
but whose meaning is not grasped by the common people,
these alien symbols become containers to be filled with the
psychic energy of the process. Hence the rituals derived from
the christian movement which are associated with birth, marriage and death, remain potent and lead, for example, to

mothers who never go to church shocking clergy by impor-
tuning them to baptise their children.

But folk religion also appears under more sophisticated
guises. When an Anglican church building is under threat of
demolition voices are raised by members of the populace
who never attend it. Our research shows that for many it has
become a religious shrine, a sacred edifice which no longer
remains the property of the institutional church, but which
just by being there now belongs to the religious life of the
local community. This interpretation gives credibility to the
remark, 'I'm not good enough to go to church', which clergy
often find irritating. For such people church is a holy place
which is devalued by their presence. One instance of this is
found in the following illustration from a village in the Mid-
lands in England, supplied by a member of the Church
Council:

> This is one of six villages whose churches are now
> administered by one vicar and his curate. Services are held
> in the six villages in rotation, and many people go to
> church each Sunday in whichever of the six churches ser-
> vices are being held. Services are taken by the vicar, the
> curate and a lay reader. Each church has its own Church
> Council, and there is also a Group Council which deals
> with affairs which affect the group.
>
> Practically nobody in the village goes to church, and
> though people travel from the other five villages for a
> service, no-one from the village itself attends. Even the
> members of the village Church Council seldom attend
> church and when a meeting of the Council is called by the
> vicar, only one or two turn up. Practically the only fre-
> quent churchgoers in the village are the children who also
> attend services in other villages.
>
> In spite of this non-use of the church, the villagers have
> maintained the church building and its graveyard over the
> years, and when the church tower needed repairing, the
> whole village worked and contributed so that this could be
> done. The heating failed but there was no difficulty in
> getting it seen to. In other words, while there are obvious
> economic and practical reasons why the church should be

closed down, it continues to be maintained by a community which does not wish to make use of it. This situation has persisted for thirty years.

The local community use the church in this manner because it is *there*, enshrining the dominant religious symbols of their culture. For such people, if their culture happened to be Indian or Arab, for example, they would look for other symbols such as Hindu shrines or Moslem mosques.

These symbols which are used in a credulous, superstitious or unreflective manner extend beyond the church building. They include its furnishings, altar/communion table, sanctuary, Bible, cross, pulpit, statues, relics, sacraments, liturgical language, creed and rituals.

One indication of dysfunctional behaviour is the resistance to change (*eg* a substitution of a new liturgical form; or the removal of a so-called 'relic' from a church). A graphic example of the latter comes from Italy concerning the *Sposa Bianca* (White Bride):

The body of a young woman killed in a railway accident in 1939 was kept in the church cemetery at Torre Annunziata, a few miles from Naples. Nothing is known of her: at the time of the accident she was carrying no documents and her only piece of luggage was a suitcase containing a new bridal gown, in which she was subsequently buried. Some years later the body was exhumed and found to be relatively incorrupt. This fact, added to the popular religious sentiment regarding her tragic death, was enough to render the body worthy of special veneration which took the form of pilgrimages and offerings. The new cult soon reached such fanatical proportions that the Archbishop of Naples felt obliged to declare it spurious and to order the removal of the body. However the devotees of the *Sposa Bianca* reacted with such determination that he decided to accept the lesser of the two evils: to tolerate the cult rather than alienate a large mass of pious faithful (Emanuel, 1977, p. 356).

Our hypothesis is that the regression to a 'lower' stratum

of consciousness in S-activity has released such psychic energy and emotions in people that they have lost control and projected their images drawn from their unconscious on to objects and turned them into sacred symbols. For Britain today the symbols of the christian movement are sacralised by the people rooted in the cultural process, thereby ignoring the significance that the church or clergy attach to them.

But before Christians inveigh against these people and dismiss their behaviour they need to pause and consider several points. The first is that those who as christian believers feel committed to apostolic religion can and do revert to folk religious behaviour from time to time, for example by hanging St Christopher medals in their cars, opening up the Bible at random to find guidance, or wearing a cross for protection.

Secondly the christian movement has expanded by taking over existing sacred places and transformed them into symbols of the movement. So temples dedicated to the Greek gods were turned into christian churches of which there is an excellent example in Syracuse, Sicily. Pagan feast days were baptised as christian festivals, for example Christmas and Easter. The introduction of Christianity into Britain was consolidated by the early missionaries taking over the existing pagan sanctuaries such as Iona and Lindisfarne. The following extract from Bede (1955 edition, p. 86) makes this same point. He is quoting a letter from Pope Gregory to the Abbot Millitus on his departure for Britain (AD 601):

> Therefore, when by God's help you meet our beloved brother, Bishop Augustine (of Canterbury), we wish you to inform him that we have been giving careful thought to the affairs of the English, and have come to the conclusion that the temples of the idols in that country should on no account be destroyed. He is to destroy the idols, but the temples themselves are to be aspersed with holy water, altars set up, and relics enclosed in them. For if these temples are well built, they are to be purified from devil-worship, and dedicated to the service of the true God. In this way, we hope that the people, seeing that its temples are not destroyed, may abandon idolatry and resort to

these places as before, and may come to know and adore the true God. And since they have a custom of sacrificing many oxen to devils, let some other solemnity be substituted in its place, such as a day of Dedication, or the Festivals of the holy martyrs whose relics are enshrined there.

This leads towards the conclusion that a new movement is successful when it offers a more potent symbolic language to satisfy the urges which derive from process. If folk religion is flourishing through utilising christian symbols then those who still consider these symbols have power, may have more to learn about their movement and themselves than by condemning folk religion. The freedom people have to put their own interpretation on christian symbols, interpretations based on instincts for survival, for fertility and for manipulation of others, which had hitherto been kept underground, show how the christian meanings have lost their potency. Superstitions emerge openly from the caves and hollows of the minds of the general mass of the people, and the old symbols get new meanings, so that for example to wear a cross today is not necessarily to intend any christian significance.

Thirdly the churches might regret their hastiness in turning away those wanting to utilise christian symbolism dysfunctionally. At least it kept open a channel of common ritual language so that Christianity could be and remain part of the psychic process of society. Other symbolic forms are close to hand, and possibly because they have few or no moral sanctions attached to them they are that much more attractive; witchcraft and astrology are examples. People who formerly sought supernatural guidance and support from the daily biblical text in newspapers, now look for their future from the stars and the planets on the astrological page. Immigration into Britain from Asia, Africa and the West Indies increases the number of alternatives available especially when it is reinforced by enquiries into the disciplines and practices of Eastern cults of personal consciousness such as Yoga and Zen.

Because folk religion is essentially concerned with process and not movement its devotees do not concern themselves with truth and logic, or reflect upon the validity of their belief. Their concern, if any, when they participate in the ritual is whether it is being carried out correctly in accordance with the rubrics. Belief is 'above their heads'. Clergy and others who consider their integrity lies in ensuring the purity of faith therefore are prone to condemn folk religion harshly, and to endeavour to root it out from their midst. As we have seen it is not so easy. All it may do is to lead to a sectarianism which then becomes a new focus for folk religion; for example some strict evangelical churches show signs of a form of ancestor worship.

Because folk religion is totally unconcerned with change it presents an opportunity for those in power to exploit their position, and even to reinforce it when in times of social and political upheavals they are threatened with revolutionary changes. Folk religion robs its devotees of the perception of the potential of change for good, and deprives them of the capacity to fight against political élites who wish to obstruct change from selfish, sectarian or chauvinistic reasons. By manipulation, whether deliberate or not, the masses are fed with ideas which cause them willingly to collaborate in their own deprivation:

> The rich man in his castle,
> The poor man at his gate,
> God made them high and lowly
> And ordered their estate.[1]

This is the religion that Marx (1844) condemned as being:

> ... the sigh of the oppressed creature, the sentiment of a heartless world, and the soul of soulless conditions. It is the opium of the people.

Such religion is not imposed by threats; the people forge their own chains. But as Marx learned it takes much more

---

[1]Written by Mrs C. F. Alexander, wife of the Protestant Archbishop of Dublin.

than an appeal to rouse the masses from their addiction to their chains, it has needed bloody revolutions in many countries, to be consolidated by evolving new symbols – sacred symbols of the State, which institute an officially sponsored form of folk religion. This was clearly exemplified by Chairman Mao's Red Guards of 1966–69, where the leaders themselves were made into the pre-eminent symbols by skilful use of propaganda, as illustrated for example in the following extract from the periodical *China Reconstructs* (December 1976):

> At 10 o'clock in the morning, to the majestic strains of 'The East Is Red', Chairman Mao, the reddest, reddest sun in our hearts, appeared on the Tien An Men rostrum. 'Chairman Mao is here! Chairman Mao is here!' Thousands of emotion-filled eyes turned toward Chairman Mao! Thousands of people waved their gleaming red *Quotations from Chairman Mao Tse-tung* and shouted again and again: 'Long live Chairman Mao! Long, long live Chairman Mao!' Oh, our respected and beloved Chairman Mao, how we have longed to see you! It is you who have given us new life. It is you who have lighted the flame in our fighting youthful hearts. It is you who have led us from victory to victory. We knew that just one glimpse of you would give us greater wisdom and courage – and today our wish has come true!

While the state of affairs just described may be inapplicable to Britain and the rest of the western world the voice of Marx can be heard more clearly than it was in 1849 when the Communist Manifesto was published. For christian leaders its message is probably more pertinent than all the discussion about christian unity and ecclesiastical re-organisation. It poses the question of the churches' accountability to the State for the religion it fosters. The strategy we advocate is for the churches to examine if, as we have hypothesised, they are the embodiment of a symbolic relation between process and movement. If they are not then there is nothing further for us to say, but if they are, they had better accept responsibility for all the citizens of their own State, whether or not they have any christian alignment, and take seriously anyone who wishes to use the services of the churches for whatever reason; which brings to mind the well-known remark of William Temple, Archbishop of Canterbury: 'The church is the only institution which exists for the sake of those who do not belong to it.' It is for the churches to take folk religion on board and to see through the bizarre and sometimes repellent behaviour to the human beings who are struggling with powerful emotions even though they mostly are unaware of themselves doing it. It is a daunting task requiring leaders who know what they are doing, and we will discuss it further with reference to leadership.

Secularism

In our previous discussion (p. 87) we saw secularism as a religious type reacting strongly against dependence and advocating symbols of inter-dependence[1] and mutuality to avoid coping with leadership roles taken by individuals. To obtain New Testament sanction for this appraisal it is necessary to demythologise the teaching of Jesus and interpret it in current social and political terminology.

The contrast with folk religion is immediately evident. Folk religion is the outward expression of deep emotions which are kept unexamined through ritualisation. By contrast, secularism is the rationalisation of behaviour so as to avoid the failure of knowing how to depend on God. Our experience is that practitioners of secularism feel committed to reject all forms of dependence, and regression to dependence, even to the extent of turning down the possibility that there are several patterns of dependent conditions, such as mature, immature; resourceful, resourceless; adult, childish; and sophisticated, unsophisticated patterns of dependence. Also regression can be neurotic and psychotic, natural and healthy; there is a negative conception, and a positive conception; as a sign of childhood, as evidence of maturity; as a way

[1] Not to be confused with *intra*-dependence.

to avoid reality, as a way to discover reality; and in the service of a sick mind, and in the service of the psyche and ego.

One criticism is that secularism sets out to do a job of citizenship on the wrong premise of circumventing dependence, only to create conditions of dependence in society which it then aggravates. For example by devaluing the dependent aspects of worship to the practitioners the instigators of secularism deny them the opportunity of dealing with unresolved problems of dependence in working through the transition from extra-dependence. The consequence is that the care of the young, sick, disabled and disadvantaged has often been organised more to deal with the dependent needs of the sponsors and staff than for the benefit of the children, patients and clients. Society then becomes preoccupied with effects and not with causes. We concentrate on the problems of unemployed young people, instead of examining the whole educational system. We are becoming preoccupied with treating the symptoms of diseases, rather than eliminating their causes.

As we shall see, religion is a platform from which to prophesy against social evils and to advocate reform, but it does not provide a base from which to fight. Religious wars are the most cruel of all. Secularist religion encourages its members to see the need for changes in our society and facilitate more effective use of our collective resources, but they endeavour to use the church as the instrument of change rather than to prepare people to occupy positions of power in the secular world from where they could directly influence change. We maintain that those people who can make an effective transition from extra-dependence are those who can freely take up this base to fight against the injustice of the State in the cause of the citizens of the State, and have the insight and skill to fight over the relevant issues with the appropriate enemies. Where people engage in fight with their own dependent needs unfulfilled, they often choose the 'wrong' enemies.

But we have a more fundamental argument against secularism. It can only exist in social groups which are questioning the validity of authority. It is disallowed in dictatorships because it always wants to tell the State what to do; it cannot survive in a group where authority is vested in a trusted leader because the group symbols foster dependence on him. Inter-dependence is a powerful fantasy because it inspires hope, and we all need our share of it. But inter-dependence or 'pairing' (cf. Appendix) is self-regarding or narcissistic when each member is homogeneous with the other. They simply reinforce their initial identities and self-images, and become introverted and ultimately sterile.

In churches which are located in new housing estates, new towns, or in highly mobile communities we have almost always observed the same phenomenon although carried out with wide differences in degrees of competence. There is a Sunday morning family service or parish communion where there is a shared leadership between clergy and laity in conducting and planning the service and emphasis on the children as part of the congregation. Here are people who are new to the environment, new to one another and looking for a way to relate to their circumstances; it is manifestly an identity-seeking operation. This need is generally openly acknowledged but what may be surprising is the usual rebuttal of dependence on the clergy. In that case, if there is emphasis on the church as a spiritual community of brotherly love, the worship is exceedingly friendly but there is little awe and mystery in contemplating and worshipping God. We are reminded of Harvey Cox's early work on *The Secular City* (Cox, 1965), where God and Man were treated as co-partners. The religious symbols of the church are the projections of the human needs of restless families. In order for these symbols to be credible a mythology occurs, Jesus becomes a friend, a pal, a mate and spirituality a guarantee of a successful life. In the effort to make this fantasy into reality the church itself must be successful, and with dedication and hard work from its members it often is – or else it collapses. The church has to go on growing and expanding to maintain expectancy. They display the same psychological motivation which leads to parents having very large families.

A subsidiary theme is that of Mother Church with all her children, and the increasing use of girls in the role of acolytes and women as servers and ministers adds to this impression, although it would usually be vigorously denied by the church members in the name of equal opportunity for the sexes. The extra-dependence is kept latent.

Therefore secularism finds its energy from the denial of dependence, and can lead on to the two subsidiary pairing types, homogenous pairing leading to sterility, and heterogeneous pairing leading to over-production and superficiality. Secularism is a vote of no confidence in the Lord God Omnipotent. Therefore though it uses the traditional outward forms and ceremonies of the church the emphasis is not on the performance of the liturgy or the search for underlying meaning but on human beings in their need, individually and collectively. Worship is valued as a way of stressing those needs and for finding ways to meet them, with the more settled congregations focussing on the needs of others, and the developing congregations being conscious of their own need.

Because this religious type is derived from understanding human interactions from that human position (compare our comments on incarnation on p. 87) then such a religion is restricted by the current social, political and economic values of the environment. The hope which it extends for the ultimate survival and growth of mankind may satisfy the activists but it still leaves a large proportion of people yearning for a divine leadership which they have had taken away from them.

What we can be grateful for in secularism is the necessity it imposes on those who consider they behave in accordance with apostolic religion. They are compelled to question if their church rituals and ceremonies are blinding them to the realities of life in their human communities. It also puts pressure on clergy to ask about their leadership: has it resulted in under-developed passive men and women, who are unfitted to give any lead in changing a social structure whose complexities make the reasons for its deficiencies difficult to locate? The church needs to promote a divine humanism, but primarily that is the outcome of regeneration in extra-dependence, not education in intra-dependence.

Apostolic Religion

The mark of apostolic religion is that it can work with human experience to enable its followers to face their predicament as human beings in the context of their actual living and working. Dysfunctional religious types fail to achieve this. For example, folk religion tries to satisfy the inward emotions in a way which causes its devotees to lose touch with the realities of the external world, and the practitioners of secularism try to satisfy the needs of the environment at the expense of losing touch with their own inner world of the emotions. In both cases the true meaning of liturgy in worship is left unexplored in its depths of feeling and thought.

In describing the two modes of consciousness we identified two dimensions of human existence, one where man in his solitariness cries out for the meaning of existence, and the other where he struggles to exist as one among many. Apostolic religion seeks to provide opportunities for its followers to express their inner solitariness in the corporate worship of God, so that they become one with other human beings in working out how to live together and share the human and material resources they have at their disposal.

Functional apostolic religion is manifested in its results – in the welfare of the social system in which it is practised, and in the development of that social system in response to the challenge of new conditions, its enrichment, its enlightenment and its enjoyment. We may know what constitutes functional religious behaviour in a church – the control of the regression, the character of the god evoked in worship, but our conclusions must always submit to the test of what happens outside the church, temple or shrine. Within the christian movement there is a strong tradition that: 'by their fruits you shall know them' (Matt.7:20). The prophets asserted that all the ritual sacrifices and offerings in the temple are rendered null and void because the misery of the poor persists amid the luxury of the cynical rich. The judgment of the religious attitudes and integrity of the temple worshippers requires no in-depth analysis, for it is made plain by their good or bad fruits in the conduct of society as a whole. The New Testament describes how the early churches were embroiled in confusion and controversy about the primacy to be assigned to 'faith' or 'good works', as justifying the person before God. The letter of James reiterates this prophetic principle. Paul's letters go one step further and show his approach to the debate was to insist that altruistic acts, or good works, performed in order to obtain God's approval were not only ineffective in gaining that, but were dehumanising to the recipients because they were not motivated by love. They are certainly not the means by which social needs are truly met; religious acts (so-called) are not instruments of social change.

For members of a local church this is confronting them with a dilemma. It suggests they had better concentrate on worshipping God in church and on the priestly and pastoral work which promotes this, so that outside they will be prepared to become wholly absorbed in being occupied with the affairs of humanity. But if so, what about the usual church programme of activities which they believe are essential for the life of the church? It could be maintained that since local churches are largely voluntary societies they rely on busy men and women donating some of their leisure time, sometimes sacrificially, to organise and finance the church, so we have parochial church councils, stewards meetings, vestry meetings and boards of management. The preparation of the service and its music generally requires the participation of volunteers. Those who attend Sunday worship cannot reasonably be expected to obtain sufficient spiritual sustenance unless they have further opportunities to discuss and argue and pray over their faith and find support for its application in practice. Children do not generally receive adequate christian education from home or school and unless their church does something they will remain spiritually immature and illiterate. The church as the Body of Christ is called to witness and mission in his name, so preparation time, and opportunities for presentation must be found sometime during the week. Church members are often strangers to each other, coming as they do from different neighbourhoods and from diverse backgrounds, so they need to meet and develop a common fellowship. Committees and working parties need to plan the way the church will carry out its social responsibility to the community. Local church representatives are invited to sit on synods and councils of the churches at dis-

trict, deanery, diocesan and national levels in order to formulate and care for the policies of the churches as institutions.

We need to ask why the churches in our time have
sprouted these multifarious activities when compared with
churches from past centuries. This is not the place for detailed
examination but one or two features deserve attention. We
suggest the fundamental factor is the change from the conditions where one religious institution was dominant in a social
entity to the current pluralistic situation where many religious institutions vie for attention from the members of that
social entity. Where one religious institution is dominant
there is no clear boundary between practitioners and non-
practitioners of religious behaviour; in England everyone
was automatically 'C of E' unless they opted out. Consequently church festivals were also national festivals and vice
versa. On gala days the churches were involved as key participants in bringing forth their symbols and treasures for
public reverence and rejoicing, or recrimination.

By contrast where one social group contains many religious institutions, boundaries are clearly drawn. Within those
boundaries the churches have their own life styles expressed
not only in their conduct of worship but developed through
their extra-liturgical activities. Their purpose is to generate
attachment to a form of religious institution as embodied in
that particular local church, against the rival claims of other
religious institutions. Two things follow: first, leaders of the
churches of different denominations become so preoccupied
with justifying their separate identity over other religious
groups in seeking to build larger churches and extend their
programmes that they are reduced to paying lip service to
their common identity with other christian groups. Their
squabbles about the authentic way to interpret the christian
movement have the effect of ceasing to provide a coherence
which can regulate the nation's oscillation process. These
local churches begin to operate on the fantasy that they are
self-contained societies with their own values, norms and
morals, and in so doing leave the populace in the lurch. Secondly, the populace feels remote from religious institutions
as presented by the various churches and people begin to look
for other ways of meeting their needs when they regress to

extra-dependence, which causes them to develop syncretistic cults and rituals, frequently re-interpreting the symbolism which they had hitherto seen in terms of the christian movement. Once this tendency takes hold, even if the churches amalgamate and submerge their denominational loyalties, they are unlikely to reverse it.

This line of reasoning causes us to be sceptical about the authentic nature of the proliferation of groups and clubs in local churches. Robert Merton (1963), speaking of systems of activity, distinguishes two kinds of function, manifest function and latent function. The manifest function of the activities of the local church apart from those devoted to worship, the preaching of the Word and the ministry of the sacraments, and pastoral care in times of transition or crisis, is to edify and maintain the members of the church, but their latent function may be to preserve it against assaults and erosions caused by forces originating from the environment. The church members see only the manifest function, but if our supposition is correct, people outside the church will be affected by the latent function which erects a barrier against them.

On the basis of our hypothesis that the task of apostolic religion is to facilitate the oscillation process in order that the social environment might exhibit the marks of well-being and development (Emery and Trist, 1973), our conclusion is that the function of the local church which facilitates interaction with the environment is of more importance than the function which turns the church members in on themselves, however spiritual and worthy those activities may be. In this light the present day activist church programmes are more like reactions to contemporary pluralistic sub-cultures than the growth of new insights into the mission of the people of God. In social systems where political policy maintained or tolerated slavery, the plea 'let my people go' was addressed to Pharaoh of Egypt, or to the Southern States of America; but under the regime of pluralism perhaps the State could be asking the same question of the churches, claiming they are of more use in their role of citizen than in their role as members of church clubs.

Functional religious behaviour is centred around the recognition of the immediacy of life. Unless the issues of the 'here and now' can be faced, the 'there and then' cannot be properly understood; a point made in the Fourth Gospel where Jesus reiterates in his claims of I AM, the living God of the Old Testament. Apostolic religion is like manna, it cannot be kept from one week to the next. A church congregation which gets at this issue by trying to understand the question what it *is* doing, rather than what it *should* be doing, will probably discover for itself how to cope with the dilemma concerning the extent of its own activities. Beyond stating certain principles an outsider to a specific situation cannot go. We can only hope that the open-ended character of the above question will stir up members of religious groups to be relentless in searching for evidence from their own experience.

One test of apostolic religion as it appears in the local church is its image of God, and its account of man's relationship with him. Are the worshippers' fantasies of their own condition and needs, and the god they want, caught and moulded by the images of the person and work of Jesus Christ who was crucified under Pontius Pilate, who originated the movement to which every christian gathering is heir? Or do they take over these images and use them for different purposes? Every organised initiative towards renewal in the churches is in some way the effort to rescue these true images from the accretions of folk religion and the depletions of secularism. But on a smaller scale every believer is asked to do the same thing every Sunday when he submits his own symbolic fantasies of S-activity in extra-dependence to the discipline of the liturgy.

Another test is whether the local church regards itself as accountable for the quality of life sustained by its social environment. In the first place do the members of the church see themselves as fully participating members of the working environment and its civil institutions, and do they accept that their church is one social/human institution with a contribution to make to the whole, in comparable ways to the assessment of other institutions like schools, the police force, hospitals and local government? If the 'whole' – village, town, suburb, city or nation – being referred to is subject to breakdown or overwhelmed by disruptive behaviour, does the church referred to protest and blame other bodies, or acknowledge its accountability and seek out ways for improvement? It may scarcely be credible to conceive of football hooliganism or political corruption or pornography in these ways because many churches are so out of practice through their neglect of Amos and Isaiah.

A third test concerns the measure of responsibility the local church members acknowledge towards individuals and groups living or working in their locality. What conditions do the members impose before accepting responsibility? Does the individual have to be attached to that church? or is it enough for him to be Christian? or is the qualification needed that of being a neighbour, someone who is *there*? An example from our work among representatives of local churches in Great Britain will illustrate this issue. In the course of conducting a version of the Parish Life Conference developed in conjunction with R.W. Herrick of Chelmsford Church of England diocese, we have asked ordinary parishioners of several hundred churches whether they would feel responsible for a person in distress who lived in their parish or district but who was not necessarily linked to their, or any, church. Their response was extremely illuminating. Most groups from Church of England parishes immediately accepted responsibility, and the remainder did not need much discussion before they did likewise. When it came to the other churches it was a different matter. The Free Churches usually only accepted responsibility if the person was a member of their denomination, as did the Roman Catholic groups; some were even more exclusive and required the person to be a member of their own congregation. Very few had the same attitude as the Anglicans. The parish system has many antagonists, but here is evidence of some functional religious behaviour. We suspect that in the recent years this behaviour has been reduced in its scope because of the devaluation of parish life by some clergy and members of the hierarchy of the Church, whose action in the cause of efficiency has undermined the structures which support love and concern.

A fourth test can be made by analysing the church services themselves. Do they show any signs that what is happening in church is being carried out on behalf of the majority of persons in the locality who are not in touch with any church or anyone who attends church? One indicator is the content of the intercessions. Do they include current events of particular relevance to the neighbourhood but not necessarily to church members? Are the leaders of the social structure prayed for? and by name? In other words, would it be true that people living in the locality are, in the opinion of the worshippers, being remembered in prayer before God? Another indicator is the attitude in the service. If someone stood up and asked whether the congregation gathered there felt they were attending church on behalf of other people, what would their response be? Outright denial, uncertainty, grudging acceptance, ready acknowledgement or puzzlement at the question? Would the clergy response be positive or negative and have they ever mentioned it?

A different way of checking this issue would come up if the church had some problem which affected outsiders; if, for example the spire was badly needing repair or the church was to be declared redundant. It could be expected there would be protests about closure, and some willingness to give towards repairing the spire from complete outsiders because of their involvement in folk religion. But how do the church members respond to their reactions? If they are profoundly grateful or bewildered or annoyed then the evidence is they do not see the church as a focus of vicarious oscillation, but if they accept the outsider's assistance as they would each other's then, whether they are consciously aware or not, they are worshipping on behalf of the total community.

In advocating these four tests we need to set them alongside those which emerged in the exploration of the differences between functional and dysfunctional religious behaviour (Chapter 4), but here we have exchanged the more analytic role of the fieldworker for that of the interpreter which has something in common with the role adopted by the Old Testament prophets. There are important comparisons and differences between the world of the prophets, that of the New Testament churches and that of the local churches in the Western world. All three function(ed) amid pluralistic sub-cultures, but the Old Testament prophets could perceive an over-arching unity in the rule of Yahweh over Israel and Judah, whereas apart from in the gospel narratives about Jesus, the New Testament writers generally made much less of the rule of God in the present, that is as King, and more about him as Creator and Redeemer, except in the eschatological books such as Jude and Revelation. Probably because the surrounding Jewish and pagan sub-cultures threatened to eat up the young churches, those writing letters to the churches focussed more on the threatening aspects of their environment rather than their responsibilities and opportunities. In our own time we need to draw on the wisdom of both testaments, but if we take seriously the role of the member of the Kingdom of God (see Chapter 6) in a mostly-christianised society then as far as our outlook on the world is concerned we need to pay special heed to the old prophets. We come unstuck and degenerate into fanaticism when the passion for doctrinal purity ceases to be accompanied by a humility which continually submits to the prophetic principle, and which is sensitive to Oliver Cromwell's plea: 'I beseech you, in the bowels of Christ, think it possible you may be mistaken'. Cromwell's own actions in Ireland against the Irish show with what difficulty that humility is maintained.

To sum up, we cannot define specifically the conditions under which apostolic religion will be found, without in effect claiming to know the unknowable – that is, to know whether the conception of God which faith believes in as reality does or does not correspond to an active being who intervenes in the affairs of men; or, expressed theologically, without claiming to know where and when the Holy Spirit will work. We can however say that the religious practices which provide a compatible setting for apostolic religion are those of a church, within a social group, which is based on the recognition that the resources of the christian church which are the products of its history are the means by which the members of that social group can engage with the realities of both corporate and individual life. These resources include the Bible, the sacraments, the historic creeds and confessions, doctrinal and theological formulations, liturgies, prayers, hymns, church buildings, accounts of the lives of the Christians of the past, and works of art in paintings, sculpture, music and poetry enshrining christian experience. None of these resources can of course be accepted uncritically as a manifestation of movement, without lapsing into folk and other forms of dysfunctional religion.

Chapter 6

The Movement

In the previous chapter we gave three examples of possible relations between process and movement. In folk religion the fantasies evoked in the extra-dependent mode of the process take over the symbols of the movement. In secularism the symbols of the movement are endorsed with apparent exclusion of the fantasies of the process. In apostolic religion the symbols of the movement act as vehicles for the fantasies of the process and at the same time refine them.

These are examples of the more general proposition, that movement and process are related to one another as *container* and that which is *contained*. Movement gives form to process; process gives life to movement. Bion (1970), who employs these terms, suggests that their relationship may be symbiotic – that is, each nourishes the other – or parasitic – in which case one element weakens the other and in so doing may destroy itself. If this model is applicable to religion, as we believe it is, folk religion and secularism are in their pure form self-destructive.

So far in this study we have focused upon process, and have allowed our assumptions about movement to remain tacit or metaphorical. Our justification for this is that there have been many studies of religious movements, both from the standpoint of anthropology and sociology, and of commitment to particular systems of belief; whereas our account of the process is we believe original. We shall not therefore develop the concept of movement to the same extent, but will in this chapter explore two propositions, the first briefly, the second at greater length.

The first is that an examination of process, from its source in the life of the individual, through its manifestations in groups and communities, necessarily brings into view the psychological properties of the containing element which 'fixes' it as a social phenomenon (using the word 'fix' in the photographic sense). There is scope for extensive examination of movement from this point of view.

The second is that an examination of the doctrines of any movement may be expected to reveal, in its own theological categories, an account of the intra-dependent and extra-dependent modes, and of the relationship between them which the movement upholds. This is linked to the character of the primal object and how its relationship to the life of man is understood. We have not tested this proposition with respect to religions other than that which is the subject of this study. We believe it is demonstrable with respect to the christian religion, and to the message of Christ as depicted in the Gospels. We shall therefore, in the latter part of the chapter, present a tentative interpretation of the Gospels in these terms. We should add that we do not expect this to be accepted by all theologians, and that it is not integral to the argument of the book.

Movement as container

The containing or fixing of the process is alluded to in our earlier definition of religion, which we defined as 'a social institution which provides a setting in ritual for the regulation of the oscillation processes in a social group' (p. 52). The key word here is 'ritual', which we would link, as many other writers have done, with the words 'symbol' and 'myth'. The oscillation processes of individuals are synchronised, and the process is contained, as the ephemeral and idiosyncratic fantasies of individuals coalesce in shared conceptions represented by shared symbols. A symbol is 'any object, act, event, quality or relation which serves as a vehicle for a conception' (Clifford Geertz, following Langer (1942)). The most important symbols are those of the primal object, referred to by Langer as 'life-symbols'. Langer links symbol and ritual in this way:

With the formalization of overt behaviour in the presence

of the sacred objects, we come into the field of *ritual*. This is, so to speak, a complement to the life-symbols; for as the latter present the basic facts of human existence, the forces of generation and achievement and death, so the rites enacted at their contemplation formulate and record man's response to those supreme realities (Langer, 1957 edn. p. 153).

Ritual acts, like kneeling, eating consecrated bread, or laying hands on someone's head, do not simply express an emotion; they symbolise it, in a way which is recognised non-verbally and, in favourable circumstances, absorbed as an attitude held in intra-dependence.

A more complex and elaborated container is offered to the worshipper through myths – using this term, not in the sense of a fiction, but in the technical sense employed for example by Barbour:

Religious symbols and images are combined in the complex narratives known as myths ... Myths offer ways of ordering experience. Myths offer a world-view, a vision of the basic structure of reality (Barbour, 1974, pp. 19f).

Through myths the character and qualities of the primal object attain colour and dimension through being placed in a setting – the setting of the life of the individual, the affairs of human society, the phenomena of the natural world. The worshipper is therefore enabled to bring the preoccupations of his whole life into the act of worship, and to allow the experience of worship to permeate all his relations in the intra-dependent mode.

Symbol, ritual and myth may evolve from within the process itself, in any community or culture, or they may be introduced from outside. It is in the latter sense that we may speak most appropriately of the interaction of process and movement. We shall comment on each of these possibilities in turn.

In the first case we have in effect the situation characterised earlier as folk religion. The character of the primal object reflects the corporate experience of the tribe or community concerned, and this shared conception becomes attached to certain sacred times, places, objects and actions. In settled times there may be little or no pressure to articulate a mythology or theology. In times of change the rituals may no longer be adequate to contain and give meaning to the experiences of the community as they are reflected upon in extra-dependence. In this case the survival of the people and their religion may depend upon a prophetic initiative which reinterprets the ancient symbols or introduces new ones. This may be seen as a movement, originating within the sphere of the religion in question, after the manner of the Old Testament prophets.

It should be noted that many theories of religion take as their starting point the notion, that religious symbols and myths have arisen through the institutionalisation of fantasies of powerful and idealised figures, which men have projected on to the sky; in other words, they have arisen from the process:

> Now if horses or oxen or lions had hands to paint and make works of art that men make, then would horses give their gods horse-like forms in painting or sculpture, and oxen oxen-like forms, even each after its own kind (Xenophanes, 6th century BC, quoted by Clement of Alexandria, *Stromateis*, 5.109.2).

This is the argument of Feuerbach in *The Essence of Christianity*, who held that progress in religion takes place as 'what was formerly contemplated and worshipped as God is now perceived as something human' (quoted in Bettis, 1969, p. 127); and of Freud, who regarded gods as projections of childhood images of the father (Freud, 1927).

The word 'movement' is most clearly applicable in circumstances in which the process is regulated by symbols, rituals and myths introduced from outside the culture in question. Since there can be no process without some containing element, continuity demands that the movement does not make a clean sweep, but 'baptises' existing sites and ceremonies, introducing a new interpretation of their symbolic significance (cf. the advice of Pope Gregory, p. 104).

Many examples could be given of the incursion of a new movement into an existing religious activity, including that of Paul on Mars Hill:

So Paul, standing in the middle of the Areopagus, said: 'Men of Athens, I perceive that in every way you are very religious. For as I passed along, and observed the objects of your worship, I found also an altar with this inscription, "To an unknown god". What therefore you worship as unknown, this I proclaim to you . . . ' (Acts 17:22f).

Gilbert Murray, following Jane Harrison, interprets the evolution of Greek religion along similar lines. Commenting on the Athenian Diasia, which was held in honour of Zeus Meilichios, he says:

A god with an epithet is always suspicious, like a human being with an 'alias'. Miss Harrison's examination shows that in the rites Zeus has no place at all. Meilichios from the beginning has a fairly secure one. On some of the reliefs Meilichios appears not as a god, but as an enormous bearded snake, a well-known representation of under-world powers or dead ancestors . . .
    The Diasia was a ritual of placation, that is, of casting away various elements of pollution or danger and appeas-ing the unknown wraths of the surrounding darkness. The nearest approach to a god contained in this festival is Meilichios . . . His name means 'He of appeasement', and he is nothing else. (Murray, 1925, pp. 28ff).

Murray goes on to suggest that the first entirely an-thropomorphic conception of a god came into Greece with the invading Achaeans. Their mountain God, Zeus, 'had the extra-ordinary power of ousting or absorbing objects of aboriginal worship which he found in his path. The story of Meilichios is a common one' (Murray, 1925, p. 70). It may be impossible to know whether Zeus gained his new adherents at the point of the sword, or whether, as seems likely, his image also had an intrinsic appeal, introducing an added dimension to the worship of the Greeks. We would suppose that the willing adoption of the symbols of a new movement by a tribe or people implies that their previous forms of religious activity are no longer adequate even for maintaining the stability of their society. This view is supported by the study of small groups, in which it is found that the perceived failure of the leader of the group dominated by the dependent pattern of relatedness (see Appendix), frequently leads to a swing to the expectancy (or pairing) pattern, in which the group is held together by the hope of deliverance by a Messianic figure.

Acceptance of the symbols of the new movement may imply a perception that those of the old religion are no longer adequate vehicles for containing the life-experience of the worshippers; they are empty or bankrupt. Or it may imply that the old symbols, though still potent, have ceased to influence behaviour in the intra-dependent mode. If, for example, the mythology of the new god depicts one who is just and loves all mankind, then individuals suffering injustice will be inclined toward the new movement. This explains why poor and disadvantaged peoples are often responsive to new prophets and charismatic leaders. The challenge of a new movement is that it speaks to a tension within the individual, between his wish for security and his wish for liberty. It comes as an offer of salvation from the bondage of the present order (cf. 'salvation religions' in Weber (1922)), but a salvation which is only obtainable at the price of insecurity and conflict. The Messiah brings, not peace, but a sword.

The myths and symbols of the new movement ideally resonate with those which represent the god of the old religion ('This I proclaim to you'), while remaining 'pegged' to a wider structure which prevents their being taken over and absorbed by the process. This structure may be provided by sacred scriptures, creeds, or forms of organisation which link local leaders or priests to centres outside the local community. Where, as in the case of the early christian movement, adherents are required to make a break with the rites of other religions, the new movement may be pegged through setting up congregations or churches committed to manifesting in intra-dependence the character of the god they now worship.

In either case the conceptions of god and man underlying the symbols of the movement are perpetually exposed to being distorted by the pressure of the conceptions associated with the local folk religion. The survival of the movement depends upon withstanding this; yet if its local leaders and priests do not accept this pressure and remain open to its influence, the symbols they uphold are unlikely to remain potent for the worshippers, because they are too rigid to accommodate their projections. In this case the movement becomes a dead letter, and the process finds other vehicles of expression.

Interaction between movement and process in the New Testament period

The distorting effect of process upon movement is illustrated in the New Testament in the letters of Paul. We shall therefore use this material as an extended illustration.

Paul was clearly an advocate of a movement which originated from Jesus. However he was unlike those apostles whose base was in Jerusalem at the heart of Judaism, and for whom at first the movement was the authentication of a process which had developed through the centuries under the influence of the Law and the Prophets (See Acts 2:16ff, 3:13). Paul travelled over Asia Minor and Greece preaching and arguing about the movement in Jewish synagogues, but always he was forced to turn away from them to address the people in whose lands the Jews had settled. The characteristic Jewish response to his message was to reject his assertion that Jesus had fulfilled their Jewish messianic hopes which were being sustained by their worship of the God of Abraham, Isaac and Jacob. In Corinth this led the Jews to protest that Paul was persuading men to worship God contrary to the (Jewish) law (Acts 18:13,15). Yet right to the end he was set on incorporating the dynamic of the movement initiated by Jesus into the historic Judaistic religion (Acts 28: 23ff). But it was not to be, and whenever he was rejected, Paul then spoke to the Gentiles whose forms and objects of worship varied from city to city and region to region. Their response to his exposition of the movement was not much more encourag-

ing so far as officialdom was involved. The movement was
bitterly opposed by those who had a vested interest in maintaining the existing process. This was nowhere more clear
than in Ephesus when, with the encouragement of the idol-
making silversmiths, the Ephesians crowded into their
amphitheatre to scream that they would not allow their goddess Artemis to be replaced by what Jesus stood for (Acts
19:28). In Athens, as we have seen, he could use an incon-
spicuous altar to an unknown god to provide a text for his
sermon, only to be mocked by the intelligentsia (Acts 17:23,
32). For them the statement of the movement was merely an
outrageous philosophical argument which bypassed the process. Yet in most places where Paul and his companions visited or stayed, Luke records that some of the hearers believed
what Paul told them about Jesus. But since there was no
existing process to which they could relate their new membership of the movement, because converted Jews were cut
off from their synagogues, and the local cults were alien to
movement, they gathered themselves together in their homes
and formed churches.

The letters which Paul wrote to these churches show how
he was constantly striving to get the Christians in the various
towns and cities to work at an authentic relation between
process and movement. In his opinion some had already distorted the movement by expressing it through rituals derived
from their traditional process. The Corinthians carried on
their Bacchanalian feasts (I Cor 10:21). In Colossi the church
had assimilated the movement to a series of mystical rites
based on the local version of Hellenistic gnosticism (Col 2:20
ff). In Galatia believers were having a Jewish religious ceremony imposed on them by representatives from the
Jerusalem Christians, who assumed that believers had to be
circumcised before they could inherit the promises to Israel
(Gal 5:1 ff).

Careful reading of the Acts of the Apostles shows that the
apostles did not set out to impose uniformity on the newly-
founded churches (Acts 15:19 ff) in order to endeavour to
preserve the essence of the movement. Indeed its author
shows that Paul could be considered inconsistent because he
took vows in the Jerusalem temple which would have

undermined the movement if they had been taken in Asia Minor. He was prepared to circumcise Timothy to conform to Judaism, and thus make him acceptable to accompany him among the Jews, whereas he refused to circumcise Titus because it would have been a betrayal of the movement to the Gentiles among whom he worked (Acts 16:3f; Gal 2:3-5). In leading and guiding the believers Paul helped them to set up churches which kept the truth of the movement intact within their local cultures, a policy which inevitably affected its adaptation to the environment. For most churches it involved some social withdrawal (I Cor 10:20 but note 10:27), but for the Roman church at least, it meant acceptance of the state institutions (Rom 13:1 ff).

The tension that Paul struggled with has never been absent from the christian church. The advice Paul gave to the Galatians about the need to resist the Jewish culture should have been passed on in the last century to many of the Christians in Africa, so they could have resisted the alienating customs of the Western European colonising powers. Failure to warn the newer churches about the need to question the assumptions of their founding fathers at an early stage in missionary history, has left many of these churches with only two alternatives: either to over-react back to the earlier processes of their tribal religions and customs; or else to transform the movement into a revolutionary force, in the belief that the church structures they have had imposed on them do not represent their own needs, but are the instrument of foreign powers.

Paul applied one uniform interpretation of the christian movement to the many and diverse background processes within which he operated. But there is a different way of relating process to movement. It occurs when the nature of the process leads its participants to differ about the interpretations of the movement. No society or community is static and hence no process remains uniform. It is always in a state of becoming something else. Hence in a society which has outwardly related movement to process, the driving force of the latter is always in a fluctuating relationship with the principles of the former. Because of class structures and differences of wealth and privilege we can properly speak of sub-cultures, and of sub-processes. In Westernised society, the wealthy ruling class stressed the conformist aspect of the christian movement, while the poor idealised the movement to compensate for their despair, and other groups were stirred by its judgments on society to political activity and social reform in the name of the movement. The rise of christian non-conformity in post-Reformation England is one example of these latter groups. Despite these various emphases the members of the respective sub-processes generally acknowledged they were all subject to the same movement.

During the history of Christendom we find many more grisly examples where different interpretations of the same movement have led to acts of terrible inhumanity. Those who disrupted the accommodation between process and movement authorised by the leaders of a society, were condemned as heretics and destroyed, in the name of a Christ who was often reduced to no more than an excuse for adhering to a designated process which the so-called heretics were threatening. Or to take a contemporary instance: today, the impact of technology and of internationalism has fragmented the post-Reformation national cultures, so that people have been less able to identify and regulate the process at a corporate level. This has led to partial severance of the process from the once-prevailing christian movement, offering the possibility for new movements or for the assimilation of the existing movement to movements from non-Western cultures.

The process as symbolised within the christian movement

We suggested at the beginning of this chapter that an examination of the doctrines of any movement may be expected to reveal an account, in mythological or theological terms, of the intra-dependent and extra-dependent modes. We shall now endeavour to validate this assertion with respect to the teaching of Jesus. In the light of the preceding section it is clear that there cannot be a pure expression of the original meaning of the christian movement. The writings of the New Testament are themselves examples of the interaction of movement and process within the christian tradition, and of the ways in which Jesus and the movement he originated were interpreted. In discussing the meaning that Jesus gave to his own work we shall not therefore enter into the debate about the accessibility of the historical Jesus and his *ipsissima verba*. Our analysis is intended merely to explore those aspects of his teaching which indicate how the movement stemming from him depicts the natural process of oscillation, and the relatedness of the intra-dependent and extra-dependent modes of human life.

Death and resurrection

Our starting point is that for Jesus his own readiness to risk all, including life itself, was a measure of his belief in the centrality of the Kingdom of God. For him entry into the Kingdom of God is attained through death. These two ideas of death and the Kingdom of God span the whole of his ministry.

All the Gospels stress that for Jesus his death was a focal point in his ministry. Its meaning can be summed up in the statement in the Fourth Gospel:

> Then Jesus replied: 'The hour has come for the Son of Man to be glorified. In truth, in very truth I tell you, a grain of wheat remains a solitary grain unless it falls into the ground and dies; but if it dies, it bears a rich harvest.' (John 12:23f).

Jesus sees death as a means to produce life. His own death was not a defeat but a means of glorification, a gateway to some higher existence. The other Gospels are more explicit about his death and his conviction about the outcome:

> He began to teach them that the Son of Man had to undergo great sufferings ... to be put to death and to rise again three days afterwards. He spoke about it plainly. (Mark 8:31f)

The significance of resurrection or of a rich harvest is that the outcome is to be of the same kind as that which dies – grain or human life. It strongly suggests that we can understand that Jesus is speaking of this earthly existence although other possibilities are not excluded. Dying can be compared with our concept of regression to extra-dependence, or death *to* the world: the resurrection refers to the concept of transformation to intra-dependence, life *in* the world. Accordingly the centrality given to the acts of death and resurrection can be seen as a theological description of the psychological expression that Jesus experienced in his crucifixion and resurrection, a transition between extra-dependence and intra-dependence. We are not affirming that this was the only occasion that Jesus alternated his modes of experience. The Gospel records Jesus' attendance at synagogue 'as his custom was', his withdrawal to pray, his fantasies about the devil and angels, and his evident dependence upon God in the garden of Gethsemane (Luke 4:16; Luke 11:1; Matt 4:1ff; Luke 22:39f); all these correspond with behaviour in extra-dependence. On the other hand Jesus spoke with authority, displayed love and affection, was angry, engaged in conflict, and instructed his disciples (Luke 20:2f; Mark 10:21; Mark 3:5; Luke 11:39ff; Mark 4:34f); examples of behaviour in intra-dependence and all vivid descriptions of inter-personal behaviour.

The Kingdom of God

Throughout the Gospels, Jesus emphasises the desirability of being a member of the Kingdom of God (Matt 6:33). It has to be striven for, yet one relinquishes things for it; it cannot be observed, yet it appears (Luke 12:24f; Mark 10:28; Luke 17:20; Luke 21:29f). It is mysterious and cannot be grasped intellectually (Mark 13:32f and 4:26ff; John 3:3ff). In the Gospels, Jesus is obviously speaking about the Kingdom with something in his mind, yet he is experienced as speaking about it in parables which the masses did not understand (Mark 4:11f) (as distinct from illustration to help them to understand), though he explained things privately (Mark 4:34) to his disciples. Rumours were evidently rife about the Kingdom of which Jesus spoke; he had to stop premature anticipation of it (Luke 19:11); he was concerned to make clear those who would and could enter the Kingdom (Luke 9:62; 13:29). It is as if Jesus worked on the assumption that too early general understanding of it would affect his ministry. Its coming depended upon his death.

The questions at his trial and the superscription on the cross confirm that Pilate was aware that he was speaking about a Kingdom for the Jews (Luke 23:2ff; 23:38). The Jewish leaders had agitated because they considered him a threat to the Temple. The accusation that Jesus would destroy the Temple and rebuild it in three days was from 'false witnesses', but one part they did get right, that Jesus had said the Temple would be destroyed (Luke 21:20). It is the opinion of some New Testament scholars that the Gospels speak of the destruction of Jerusalem because it had already occurred by the time they were written. But another explanation is that the disciples, and the Gospel compilers, saw a different reason as to why the Gospels pay so much attention to the destruction of Jerusalem and the plunder of the Temple by the Romans. It was that they perceived Jesus' message as showing there was a link between the Temple of Jerusalem and the Kingdom of God.

According to our reading, the essence of Jesus' message is that the long years of Temple worship would come to an end, and be replaced by a new way which would lead to the establishment of the Kingdom of God. The outcome of this was not for the members of the Kingdom to be rewarded with riches (a Pharisaic sign of blessing) or political independence, but to be placed in the midst of a new set of human relationships. Jesus therefore could not fully expound the Kingdom (but see Luke 9:11) without metaphorically 'destroying' the Temple. By announcing its advent at the outset of his ministry, Jesus therefore was committing himself to assaulting the prevailing Jewish Temple worship:

'The time is up; the Kingdom of God is upon you; repent and believe in the Gospel!' (Mark 1:15).

How do we understand this bombshell? What good news is being referred to which his hearers are urged to believe? We wish to advance the thesis that the good news is that the Jews need no longer be burdened by the legal injunctions of the Torah concerning the complex system of animal sacrifices which were carried out in the Temple, because Jesus is announcing that he is opening up a new way to worship God. His presence *in* the world – his 'coming' whereby the mystery of God could be known by his followers (Mark 4:11) could be contrasted with the seclusion of the Temple mysteries. He himself would displace the Temple, with the result that men and women in relating to him would also form and develop creative and fulfilling relationships with one another. Jesus was not only a replacement for the Temple, he was also the archetypal *new man*.

The Gospels have these two important interwoven themes. The first is the thesis that Jesus' death as the Way to God was not to render the law and the prophets obsolete, but to fulfil them. The second theme exemplifies, by the incidents described in Jesus' life, the behaviour which is expected of the members of the Kingdom.

The Kingdom of God and salvation

The Gospel is the text of the movement. However Jesus did not stop attending synagogue or going up to the Temple. It was still for him, his 'Father's house' (Luke 19:45f). From this we see the value Jesus placed on process even when the rituals containing it were to be re-interpreted and replaced. But process alone is not enough. This was Nicodemus' error when he consulted Jesus. Hence in answer to him, Jesus comes over abruptly:

> Unless a man has been born over again, he cannot see the Kingdom of God. (John 3:3)

The other Gospels affirm the same point in slightly different words:

> Whoever does not accept the Kingdom of God like a little child will never enter it (Mark 10:15; parallels in Matt. and Luke. The reference is to newly born infants).

The Fourth Gospel indicates that this regeneration is 'of water and the Spirit' (John 3:5). Water may symbolise baptism (see above) but the Holy Spirit is the sign of regenerative power. Just as regeneration results in new life, so also does resurrection:

> You were also raised with him through faith in the working of God, who raised him from the dead. (Col 2:12; I Peter 1:4)

Paul goes on from this passage to say that:

> If then you have been raised with Christ, seek the things that are above, where Christ is, seated at the right hand of God. (Col 3:1)

that is, we are called to share the reign of God as King, and to demonstrate that we are members of the Kingdom of God.

According to the oscillation theory, the worshipper who makes the transition from extra-dependence towards intra-dependence is 'regenerated': that which was 'extra-', God, now becomes 'intra-'. As the transformation to intra-dependence takes over, W-activity becomes dominant over S-activity. But the correspondence between the resurrection/ regeneration and the transition from extra-dependence to intra-dependence goes further:

> For we are his workmanship, created in Christ Jesus for good works, which God prepared beforehand that we should walk in them. (Eph 2:10)

The objective of the new creation is good works, and these good works are described by the author in down-to-earth terms of human behaviour (Gal 5:19-23). Paul is addressing the members of the church about the King and the Kingdom. He is speaking to them about their life in intra-dependence while they are in the extra-dependent condition. This corresponds to the liturgy and the sermon today when the language of faith is used to reinforce good behaviour in the world. The new life is 'in the Spirit', and the Galatians are told to 'walk in the Spirit' by Paul (Gal 5:25). The meaning of intra-dependence is that those who are in this mode accept personal authority for what they do in society and do not opt out of their accountability to other persons for what they do. They do not feel disappointed that their fellow human beings can only see them as fellow human beings but instead consider they are fulfilling their vocation to be as Jesus was in the world. Just as the Spirit is invisible, the Kingdom is invisible.

The Kingdom of God and social and political action

The Kingdom is a mystery. It is manifest now, yet it is in the future; it is here in this life, and yet will be revealed in the life to come (Col 3:4). It is like leaven in the meal working secretly (Matt 13:33). A clue here is the incarnation of Jesus, the Word made flesh. In his person as man, Jesus expressed himself, both verbally and in action, in terms of righteousness, when he opened up to his disciples a vision of freedom and peace where men respond to each other in love. In his public life the depth of his relationship with God was normally kept in the background and hidden. As a student of mine once said:

> Jesus made such a good job of becoming man that people could not possibly believe he was God.

Only rarely were people aware of the origin of the authority they experienced in his teaching and in his signs or miracles. It puzzled both the Pharisees and Pilate (Luke 20:2; John 18:33f), in sorting out how far Jesus was a revolutionary. He refused to become a political agitator (John 18:36), but neither did he want to found a different religion. He taught openly in the Temple (Luke 22:53), and there showed his concern for the secular things of life, care for the hungry, those with mental disorders and physical incapacities, and the poor and oppressed (Luke 14:13; Mark 5:18f; Mark 1:41; Luke 6:20ff), all of which today require political and social activity. But by whom?

The story of the Last Judgment where the King separates the sheep from the goats is pertinent:

> Then the King will say to those at his right hand, 'Come, O blessed of my Father, inherit the Kingdom prepared for you from the foundation of the world; for I was hungry and you gave me food, I was thirsty and you gave me drink, I was a stranger and you welcomed me, I was naked and you clothed me, I was sick and you visited me, I was in prison and you visited me.' Then the righteous will answer him, 'Lord, when did we see thee hungry and feed thee? . . . ' And the King will answer them, 'Truly I say to you, as ye did it to one of the least of these my brethren ye did it to me.' (Matt 25:34–37,40)

Those who gave aid were members of the Kingdom, and *yet they themselves did not know it.* By their response they indicated they had not regarded their service to the sick or the poor to be a religious one. It was to them a normal human response to need. The rest of the story confirms this interpretation, because those placed on the left hand protested:

> 'Lord, when did we see thee hungry or thirsty or a stranger or naked or sick or in prison and did not minister to thee?'

They thought that to serve God involved a religious act. If they had seen and recognised Christ in rags they would have been eager to help him. The parable shows two things are effectively hidden in this life: the membership of the Kingdom of God, and the relation of the King to the needy and the oppressed. He is hidden in their flesh and blood (but see I Cor 15:50). From the human point of view we cannot see the workings either of the King or of his followers (cf. II Cor 5:16). The invisibility of his reign is to ensure that the sole motive for serving in the name of the King has to be the need of humanity, to respond to human need *as* human need. This is the realised state of intra–dependence. The member of the Kingdom takes up a 'kingly' role in entering into the political and social issues of his society as citizen.

This discussion supplies an interpretation to the obscure saying of Jesus:

> The Kingdom of God is not coming with signs to be observed; nor will they say 'Lo here it is!' or 'there!' for behold, the Kingdom of God is *entos humōn* (Luke 17:20f).

Jesus made it plain that the Kingdom is not visible. We feel there is sufficient evidence to take *entos humōn* to mean that the principle of the incarnation applies to the members of the Kingdom. Those who are regenerate are made members of the Kingdom because they are:

> ... partakers of the divine nature (II Peter 1:4).

We are affirming that, contrary to what it appears to mean at first, the context shows that the result of this partaking is to be made more completely man, to behave as mature human beings. In this state (of intra-dependence) our authority as members of the Kingdom does not depend on external supports or institutions, political, social or even ecclesiastical; it is from within, and we are wasting our time (and copying the goats), by looking longingly over our shoulder for some work to do for the church.

The Kingdom of God and the Church

The churches have become accustomed to regarding statements about the Kingdom as referring in some way to themselves. In our terms they have muddled the nature of dependence, by assuming that the desirable relations between people in the Kingdom of God are the same as those celebrated in church. As we have shown earlier, the dominant relations in the church are extra-dependence. But in a society where the Kingdom of God is present, religion needs to be put in its place as the servant of man:

> The Sabbath was made for man, not man for the Sabbath (Mark 2:28).

The task of the church is not principally to reproduce itself, but to produce members of the Kingdom – where each member is a new creation, a new man in whom Christ has been formed (Gal 4:19). It is worth pointing out that, as *men*, members of the Kingdom are therefore able to become one with humanity and provide leadership in the service of society, but if we refer to them as *Christians* we insert a dividing barrier into the Kingdom itself. The parables of the Kingdom (Mark 4:1ff; Matt 25:1ff) make it clear that it includes both good and bad, sheep and goats, and during their lives they both exist together under divine jurisdiction. Judgment is pronounced at the end, when the genuine members of the Kingdom are identified (Matt 25:31f).

Christians who make the division into 'saved' and 'lost' prematurely are bound to be church-centred and not King-dom-centred, so they can never really expose themselves as human beings, and 'empty themselves' like Jesus of their distinctiveness (Phil 2:5ff). They can be said to have at least one foot always in extra-dependence. Their religion, however spiritual it is, becomes necessarily dysfunctional. More and more they are likely to be captured within the regressive phase where they become permeated by guilty feelings. They attribute these feelings to being contaminated by the 'evil world', whereas we would suggest that it is due to their failure to devote themselves to loving their neighbour and promoting the cause of righteousness within the communities in which they live and work.

The purpose of the church is demonstrated when it enables its worshippers to enter the Kingdom of God. It achieves this by calling men to engage in a symbolic death and resurrection. As Jesus says:

If anyone wishes to be a follower of mine, he must leave self behind; day after day he must take up his cross and follow me. (Luke 9:23)

For the early church the sacraments of baptism and Holy Communion were key rituals which signified the death and rising again of worshippers as they entered into and shared

Jesus' death and resurrection (Rom 6:4f; I Cor 10:16f; cf. John 6:53f).

This argument can be tied back to the commencement of this section (p. 131). Each of the quotations about the death of Jesus has in its context the same passage:

> '... whoever cares for his own safety is lost; but if a man will let himself be lost for my sake, and for the Gospel, that man is safe'. (Mark 8:35).

The meaning is that what Jesus was about to do he invited others to do also. It is striking that the Greek word *sōsei* here translated 'is safe', not only has implications for survival and welfare, but also for growth and development (cf. p. 57). Insofar then as the church becomes a vehicle for functional religion it can be defined as an institution which shows how men and women can be incorporated into the movement that Jesus introduced, and enter into the new life which Jesus pioneered.

A theologian, Don Cupitt, puts a point of view which illustrates our discussion:

> What lies behind the idea of the resurrection of the dead? To answer that I believe we have to go back to the beginning, to Jesus' message about the Kingdom of God.
>
> The Kingdom of God is not the medieval heaven. It is not beyond the stars, not in the remote future, not a state of trance. It is something immediately present in everybody, here and now. It makes itself felt in the conflict between good and evil which is the very stuff of life. What Jesus taught was, as he put it – that time is up, the end is near, the Kingdom of God is breaking in upon human life, and to lay hold on it you have to turn, or change, or die.
>
> Jesus' message was that dying can be made a way of life. The Kingdom can only be reached through death; there is no other way to it. One has to go through a kind of ordeal in which one accepts the victory of evil, suffering and death to the point where one has tasted extinction – and then re-birth comes on the other side (Cupitt, 1976).

In terms of the hypothesis of the oscillation process, we could say that the theological state which corresponds to the intra-dependent mode is that of the Kingdom of God; and that which corresponds to the extra-dependent mode is the Church.

The idea of the unseen Kingdom has been transferred by some throughout the ages to the Church, contributing to the growth in importance of the concept of the invisible Church. Invisibility is a means of protecting idealisation. Because the Kingdom was viewed as sharing in the power and glory of the King it provided a way out from accepting the actual local churches with their weakness, impotence and sinfulness as the true Church. It appeared to them that it was impossible to conceive that God could use such poor, inadequate, foolish institutions, forgetting that Paul wrote his letters just because he did conceive it!

We can therefore say that the essence of the Church is *to be visible*, warts and all. Only by being visible can the local congregation bear witness to God by offering a way for men and women to regress to extra-dependence. But as often as church members pass from extra-dependence to intra-dependence they take up their roles as members of the Kingdom, a process which is reversed when they make the transition from intra-dependence, and regress to extra-dependence. Men cannot see the Kingdom of God. They can only see people overcoming injustice, maintaining righteousness, fostering creativity, and ensuring freedom in the way they run their homes, do their jobs, enjoy themselves and generally join in taking their responsibility for leading their society and serving their fellow men.

Summing up this discussion on movement, we can say that Jesus in founding a movement destroyed the Temple for the Jews. He displaced it. The sacred temple curtain was torn asunder, exposing that which had been called holy to common view. As far as the Jews were concerned Jesus moved the critical arena of human life to somewhere which was 'profane', literally, 'outside the temple'. Sacredness was reserved for that area where symbolically men died to live again – the church – where men and women came to join in the ritual acts celebrating the mission of Jesus.

PART TWO

Chapter 7

The Local Church as an Institutional Setting for Religion

Because of the necessity to regulate the natural oscillation process, every human group evolves its own religion, and this in turn develops an institutional structure, formal or informal, through which myths and symbols are rehearsed and dramatised by its members. In many countries, particularly those which comprise western industrialised society, the symbols of the natural religion – the process – have been reinterpreted (*eg* the midwinter solstice by the birth of Jesus), transformed (*eg* temples have become churches) or replaced (*eg* the goddess Easter has been superseded by Christ, the Son of God) by the symbolic world of a religion from outside their cultures – the movement. The local church is the institution in which these two elements converge and interact. It is a kind of melting pot which sometimes produces the finely tempered blade of the 'sword of truth', and sometimes the devious blandishments of a witches' brew.

In concentrating upon the religious behaviour of individuals and groups personally involved in the flow of the oscillation process in earlier chapters, we have assumed the existence of an institution to provide the necessary human and material resources for these persons to utilise. As we proceed to examine the nature of the local church institution and the systems by which it deploys its resources it seems reasonable to make a further assumption.

Very few local churches would be consciously and deliberately organised to monitor the oscillation process by coping with the extra-dependent needs of a social group, by working with some of its members, so that the group as a whole might display the qualities of a healthy and free society. In our studies of local churches in Britain and elsewhere we have come across many versions of the purpose of the churches but not this one. Those we have encountered could be located on a continuum which at one limit sees the church's purpose or mission as the eternal salvation of the individual, and at the other limit the present salvation of society, with many different combinations of these two extreme positions. One such typical fusion could be stated as: the mission of the Church as the Body of Christ is to be present in the world so that men and women may respond to his love by accepting his redemption to the glory of God and the benefit of humanity.

It is our contention that whatever is the stated purpose of the local church, it is contributing in some way to the oscillation process, whether functionally or dysfunctionally, despite lack of awareness of both clergy and congregation. Following Merton (1963) again, the stated purpose can be defined as the *manifest function*, and the monitoring of the extra-dependent mode of the oscillation process, the *latent function*. We can illustrate the difference by a simple analogy. If bees could talk, and we came across them busy in a flower garden and enquired what they were doing, their reply might be: 'Gathering nectar to make honey.' But if we asked the gardener, he would almost certainly answer: 'They are cross-pollenating my flowers.' In carrying out their manifest function to make food, the bees were performing a latent function of fertilising flowers. The mutual dependence of bees and flowers is an analogue of churches and society.

We have endeavoured to show that though the efforts of church members, both clergy and laity, are mostly devoted to the manifest function, it is the latent function of the churches which is of overwhelming importance. This judgment means that once a local church ceases to contribute to the latent function then its continuance is of no interest to society. It has become nothing more than a private club looking for subscribers. In Britain it may explain why ancient church buildings of the Church of England under threat of closure arouse widespread protests while Free Church chapels can become warehouses without a murmur from outsiders. In the United States because church buildings are frequently seen in fantasy as tents of settlers, when the members move into outer suburbs they 'take' their building with them and erect another church.

A key concept in tying latent function into organisational theory is A. K. Rice's concept of *primary task* which he defines in his later writings as that task which at any given time an enterprise must perform if it is to survive (Rice, 1963). The alternative wording of Eric Trist (Trist *et al.* 1963) helps to pin the concept: 'the key transaction which relates the operating group to its environment and allows it to maintain the steady state'. The primary task of an enterprise as thus defined, is a function of its environment as well as of its internal structuring. It is a task which provides both enterprise and environment with a pay-off. (See also Reed and Palmer, 1976, p. 276f, for additional comments on this concept).

As such, primary task has to be distinguished from the *aims* or purposes entertained by members of an enterprise, and as we have said (Reed and Palmer, 1976, p. 277):

These aims need not necessarily be realised, and cannot be realised if a complementary environment cannot be found. The aims of individuals can only be realised through activities which relate institutions to reciprocating environments. The tasks which they are in reality able to perform are therefore in part determined by the 'bargain' which the environment strikes with the institution. Enterprise and environment each seek to shape the transactions between them to fit the goals which they seek to achieve.

The distinction between aim and primary task is important in any consideration of the activities of churches. Clergy and laity have hopes and ideals for the church which are often entertained with great passion. They find it correspondingly difficult to acknowledge that what actually happens in their churches is an expression not only of these aims ...

but also of the conditions of individuals and groups which go to make up its environment, which include both their conscious aims and their unconscious emotional needs.

Therefore the latent function is described through the primary task definition, and the manifest function through the statement of aim and purpose. The aims of the churches are derived almost exclusively from the christian movement; their primary task from that of the process as interpreted by the movement. Adequate primary task performance results in functional religion, inadequate performance in dysfunctional religion.

A danger lurks in the above descriptions of the primary task concept in the use of the words 'survive' and 'steady state'. They suggest that religion (and its institutions) is most effective when it is in equilibrium with its social and political environment and that functional religion promotes this balance. That pioneer of open systems theory, L. von Bertalanffy (1968, p. 191), points up the issue:

> Biologically life is not maintenance or restoration of equilibrium but is essentially the maintenance of disequilibrium, as the doctrine of open systems reveals. Reaching equilibrium means death and decay.

From their other writings both Rice and Trist show that they would accept this qualification of their concept. It demonstrates the necessity for the movement, for without it the process remains at a level of activity where it maintains equilibrium with its environment, as in the primitive forms of folk religion in isolated tribes. Apostolic religion only survives if it is able to sustain disequilibrium.

The primary task of the local church

The primary task of each local church is different and can only be defined by examining the realities of that particular church in its own environment on a stated occasion, and such detailed analysis would be outside the limits of this book. Hence we can only hypothesise about a primary task based on our field work, and hope that others will test it out for themselves against their experience of local churches. We suggest that the primary task of a Church of England parish church whose congregation is drawn mainly from within the parish (overall a usual state of affairs in England) can be defined as:

> To monitor the oscillation process by containing or rendering manageable anxieties associated with the activities of the profane world so that individuals and institutions are able to carry out the tasks on which the survival and well-being of their social group depends.

This is a general model which provides a basis for the examination of the activities of any church, Anglican or otherwise. There is no assumption made about the functionalism or dysfunctionalism of religious behaviour.

The diagram provides a model of the system of activity which performs the work which converts an input into an output in any institution:

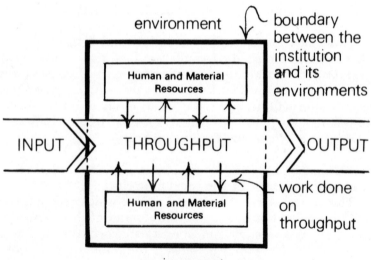

Diagram 2   **Model of task system of activity**

Applying this model to the church, the throughput is the members and other actual users of the church resources. At the input stage they are already in some regression to extra-dependence otherwise they would not be 'going to church', or consulting the vicar; they are carrying the anxieties and feelings of themselves and others from the transition from intra-dependence. As output they are in the phase of trans-formation to intra-dependence. The work needed is to con-vert the input to an output by controlling the regression in the extra-dependence mode, and facilitating the transition from extra-dependence. The activities largely responsible for this conversion process have already been summed up as centred on the worship of God (p. 71) in terms of religious behaviour.

Here we analyse that worship in terms of corporate activities which use the resources available to the church (see p. 119), at the centre of which is the traditional 'ministry of the Word (the Bible) and the sacraments'. This ministry would include for an Anglican church: morning and evening prayer, Holy Communion, preaching/teaching, baptism, confirmation, matrimony, care of sick and dying and burial of the dead.

In the 1662 Book of Common Prayer there is clear evi-dence of the cyclic nature of these activities – daily, weekly, monthly (in the Psalter), yearly – and, by providing special services, of its recognition of the crisis transitional points in life: birth, puberty, marriage and death. Within the context of the worship of God, the principal fast and feast days of the christian year focus on the oscillation process: Advent on the transition from intra-dependence (*ie* judgment and promise); Christmas on bringing together in one extra-dependence and intra-dependence (*ie* God's loving provision and the hope of creation respectively, which Epiphany reinforces); Lent on the regression to extra-dependence (*ie* repentence and self-denial); Easter on the transition from extra-dependence (*ie* the resurrection life); Whitsunday and Pentecost on the transformation in intra-dependence (*ie* the Holy Spirit bestowed on the church in the world).

At present churches everywhere are reassessing the useful-ness of those resources which comprise their inheritance from the past. If churches are healthy they will flourish on the brink of such uncertainties about their importance and will insist on testing their resources on the basis of a contemporary evaluation of the past from which they originated. We consider that much reassessment is based on mistaken advocacy of types of dysfunctional religion such as secularism and ecclesiasticism, as distinct from being sensitive to the felt needs of the people they serve. The clarification of Elizabethan terminology in Bible and Prayer Book is laudable, but the mystery and vitality of worship can be easily dissipated in the name of simplification. The promotion of 'instant worship' to make services attractive to the unchurched and to children has the effect of denying the struggle to come face to face with God. The liturgy is like a great symphony and requires the same concentrated attention, for there would be few who would claim the capacity instantly to enter into the depths of the *Missa Solemnis* of Beethoven, which demands of most of us hard and disciplined listening to competent musicians over many performances. Alas there are not many clergy who treat their fellow-worshippers with such maturity and expect them to build up their appreciation of the service over months and years, and thereby do not subject them to undue pressure or impatience. The essence of the liturgy is that it is not 'new' but 'renewed'. Its purpose is to rehearse a given symbolic language which resonates with the surrounding culture. As the culture changes due to technological and political upheavals so the settings of the symbols will need to be renewed, causing each nation over a period inevitably to develop its own religious forms. With the decreasing coherence of western Christendom and the development of the Third World, the Roman Catholic Church has, in our opinion, wisely acceded to this principle. Local churches affiliated to the same denominational structures may reflect cultural differences. American churches in black areas reflect the emotional needs of the worshippers by being more colourful and elaborate in their ceremonial than sister churches in white areas. Even the same church can cater for different strata from the same local community; for example the early 8 a.m. Holy Communion service for people sure of themselves and often leaders in the community, such as doctors, senior executives, civil servants and head teachers (who may be considered as worshipping on behalf of their clients and constituencies); and the 9.30 a.m. Parish Communion for young parents and their children, whose hopes for the future are threatened by their doubts about their identities, which cause them to look to one another for support. Forced amalgamation of these services in the name of efficiency or a concept of unity will achieve nothing because there are major differences in the fantasies associated with the services which first need acknowledgement.

By contrast with the liturgy, preaching needs to be instant – 'a word in season'. Only if the preached Word can be alive and powerful so that it quickens the given liturgy can liturgy generate its authority through its timelessness. What we understand by preaching can be clarified by reference to Diagram 2. The person preaching is required to stand on the boundary between the service and the environment from which the worshippers come, and to which they will go. Preaching or proclamation is the interpretation of the symbolic extra-dependence mode in terms of the values of the worshippers and their world. Following in the tradition of the apostles it is the proclamation of the mighty acts of God. It is, to put it crudely, 'an aid to digestion' of the Word of God and the sacraments. It takes place in the context of extra-dependence when S-activity is dominant: effective preaching therefore attracts and encourages the mind to feel around the fantasy symbols, to appreciate their potency and threats so that once internalised in intra-dependence they can affect the hearer's perceptions and judgments. Preaching is unreliable as a guide to decision-making which demands the dominance of W-activity. We made a note of a story from a church in Washington DC which illustrates this:

With a glint of amusement in his eye, the Rector told me that the greatest sermon he had ever heard in his life was preached by a woman lay member citing all the Biblical reasons why the church community should not buy a new pipe organ. He told me that at the congregational meeting following that service, all the speakers rose to compliment her on a tremendous sermon following which the congregation voted three to one in favour of the purchase of a new organ.

Augustine of Hippo said 'add the Word to the elements and a sacrament is made'. Preaching which we would consider to be functional/apostolic has this purpose. Like the words of consecration in communion it shows the symbolic values within the plain facts of life and transfigures them.

A priest who had decided to move to another parish was trying to work out how to announce this to the congregation. He felt it was going to be difficult to leave for, in a parish with an elderly population, many people had become very dependent on him because he had taken the funerals of their wives or husbands. It was suggested to him that, after announcing that he was leaving the parish in the notices, he should preach a sermon on what it was like to be left behind, perhaps taking as his text our Lord's words, 'It is expedient for you that I go away.' This suggestion started him thinking deeply about the feelings of the disciples which Jesus recognised, and about the way members of the congregation felt when they heard he was leaving. In the end he preached on John 16:6f: 'Because I have said this to you, sorrow has filled your heart. Nevertheless I tell you the truth: it is expedient for you that I go away,' and in the sermon he explored the feelings of sadness, anger and betrayal aroused by his decision to leave.

The preacher gives the myths of the christian movement authority by showing how they comprehend the depths of the human predicament while simultaneously displaying the omnicompetent qualities of God the divine leader and Father. Thus through the holding forth of biblical stories through preaching, the partaking in the Eucharist becomes the outward sign of the inward grace, where the same position from which the worshipper expressed his dependence on God for redemption becomes the regenerative spot whence the transition from that expressed dependence is operative.

But there are services with no Communion or Mass, with no set liturgy. In many Free Churches and non-Anglican services, the sermon takes the place of the sacrament where the preacher rehearses the apostolic symbols. Instead of the whole congregation overtly engaging in celebrating the myth in ceremony, the acting out has been restricted to the preacher. Under these conditions the hymn and prayers have often been window-dressing for the central event, except where the prayers have been another sermon! The Church of England service of morning or evening prayer consists of liturgical sequences which concentrate more on the need for regression and how it is controlled. It makes no effort to work at the transition from extra-dependence, but sets up a rhythm of oscillation, although in a lower key than Holy Communion. Simplicity is its strength and there is some dissonance with preaching, which either will dominate the liturgy or else be reduced to comparative irrelevancy.

Poor preaching is that which does not allow for the dominance of S-activity in which language is multivocal, that is, in which there are as many meanings attributed to the words as there are emotions aroused. The preacher fails to appreciate that listeners in extra-dependence can readily respond symbolically to God and to conceptions about themselves in relation to God, as Shepherd, Creator; but not realistically about their response to the outside world, as illustrated above. Therefore sermons which direct attention to social and political issues would be usually more effective delivered from public platforms than from pulpits.

Certain forms of evangelistic preaching flourish in worship – particularly presentations where the sin of the individual is stressed. The appeal is to engage deliberately in the regression phase, that is, at the input of Diagram 2. If the effect is limited only to this aspect of the oscillation process then the regression it induces easily gets out of control, and either leads to fanaticism, where its disciples have the fantasy that the more they display their dependence on God for forgiveness the more spiritual they are; or it fosters ecclesiasticism, because it is deficient in working through the transition from extra-dependence, and in fantasy keeps those who respond in church continually.

Sometimes evangelists devote their efforts to young people, or lonely or distressed persons whose management of the regression phase is shaky and uncertain. By their precision in spelling out the steps to be taken in approaching God, their hearers easily substitute a feeling of dependence on the techniques for dependence upon God. If the preacher is able to appreciate the corporate aspects of worship he may avoid this displacement by drawing attention to the church which despite the diversity of its members and their experience can worship God in unity through the Holy Spirit.

Teaching is to be differentiated from preaching. The latter rehearses the myths and works with the symbolic rituals. It is the task of the teacher which comes from the Holy Spirit as we are using the term to enable the would-be worshipper to understand the language of christian symbolism. Some teaching is almost inevitably included in preaching and diligent churchgoers may even consider they receive sufficient teaching through the ministry of the Word and sacraments. However teaching is a discrete task to be carried out in non-worship settings such as classes for confirmation or preparation for church membership, or outside the church environment at home or in educational establishments. As a learning activity it requires the dominance of W-activity in the intra-dependent mode, and should therefore be clearly designated as instruction in worship, bearing in mind that its effectiveness can be judged by the way it prepares individuals for worship. Thus it is more a part of the service system of the church, than of the operating system.

Other activities of a local church deriving from the ministry of the Word and sacraments are mainly concerned with transitions in life: from non-being to being – baptism; from child to adult – confirmation; from one family to another – matrimony; from sickness to health – pastoral care of the sick; from life to death – care of the dying, and burial of the dead. By the way they respond to requests on these occasions, the members of a local church reveal their understanding or lack of appreciation of the responsibility of the church to the surrounding population. If the local church concentrates upon maintaining itself and preserving its own image of itself, then the task systems devised for each of these activities will exclude those families who do not conform to the church's requirements. Babies will not be baptised unless parents promise to attend church, for example. However, if a church accepts that it has a duty to supply religious facilities to those who live in its sphere of influence just because it is there, and they are there, then church members have to endure tension and uncertainty in trying to carry out the primary task of their church. The skill required in designing appropriate task systems is very considerable. Put briefly, it involves reinforcing the importance of the regression to the extra-dependence phase for those who have requested the church's services; insight on the part of the leaders of the task system into the symbolic images and activity assumed in this regression, and their ability to create a dependable framework of liturgy and ministry whereby those engaged in the worship have the opportunity, but not the necessity, to control their regression and reinterpret their dysfunctional S-activity in symbols of apostolic religion. Pursuing this policy, the local church will not concern itself whether it is labelled rigorist or permissive because it is absorbed in concentrating its energies on being open to the cultural environment and the toleration of the disequilibrium that follows. Unfortunately the local church may be more aware of its multi-denominational environment and plan its activities to suit those demands, leaving non-members in the lurch either by neglect or by imposing impossible demands.

Each local church will have its own version of these activities. They constitute what are called the *operating system* in that they carry out the primary task of the local church institution. Institutions require three other major types of system of activity: a regulating system, a service system and a control system (for these terms, see Rice, 1963, and Miller and Rice, 1967).

The *regulating system*, as its name implies, is designed to regulate the inputs and outputs of the operating system as well as regulating the interaction between the institution and its environments. It also regulates the relations between subsystems within the institution and the goals of the various constituent systems. Therefore another name for it is the managing system because it defines local policy. In an Anglican parish church the managing system involves the entire church membership who delegate their authority to a board or committee of officers whom they elect. Other churches like the Methodists have only limited powers at local church level which are delegated from district level by the Superintendent. In the United States many local churches vest the authority of the membership in the minister or rector, but can readily strip him of his office so that his regulating function is confined within certain limits tacitly accepted by both parties.

The *service system* consists of those activities which facilitate the performance of the operating system. In this sense the organist and choir form a service system. Other examples include christian education, discussion, prayer and Bible study groups whose aim is to prepare for the service or follow it up, and task forces which assist in the planning and presentation of the services. Such groups are often tempted to take over the operating system, an indicator of which is when group members feel that if they work for the group they need not attend church or do not regard it as more than the tip of the iceberg. Proliferation of service activities can mean that the operating system is failing in its task.

The *control system* administers the use of the institution's resources and makes it aware of the constraints on task performance (*eg* finance and general purpose committees). This system may overlap both regulating and service systems, causing conflict particularly where the local church relies on the financial support of its own members. The leaders of the operating system may want to initiate changes in worship services, but be blocked by the control system's influence on the regulating system. A stewardship committee may begin by being a service system but end up as a control system; hence it is successful because of the policy on which it has based its fund raising. Control systems may not have much generally recognised authority but their power can dominate an institution, and be a dampener on initiative.

Before we investigate the leadership of these systems we wish to put forward another model of a local church institution and to compare and contrast it with the type of local parish church affiliated with the Church of England.

Communal and associational types

The assumption underlying our earlier definition of the primary task of the local church (p. 148), was that its members could be seen as drawn from a surrounding parish. Other people living in the parish could therefore be represented by those who attended church: a woman might be seen as going on behalf of her neighbours, for example, or a child on behalf of its parents. Others might participate in the life of the church vicariously, so that a worker worshipped on behalf of his department, or a policeman on behalf of the people on his beat (see p. 55). We have called this a *communal church*, because its members have an implicit shared idea about their parish as a community for which they have some responsibility. In many churches the members do not have this shared idea. They are drawn from a wide area, choosing to associate with others who share the idea that this church will endorse their convictions or meet their needs. This we have called an *associational church*. (Cf. the well-known sociological distinction between 'church' and 'sect' of Weber (1922) and Troeltsch (1931); and the elaborations and criticisms of this, for example of Martin (1962) and Wilson (1963)).

By comparing the activities and structures of these two types of church we can summarise a number of their organisational features, which reflect the differing relationships of the churches with their environments. These are not rigid distinctions: many actual churches will be found to combine features of both models:

1. *Environment*

When the environment is uniform and orderly then there will probably be a communal church (*eg* rural Church of England parish churches, Roman Catholic churches in the Republic of Ireland).

When the environment is pluralistic and turbulent then there will be associational churches offering many options (*eg* pentecostal churches, Church of England churches of extreme churchmanship, United States churches in urban areas).

2. *Membership*

For communal churches, membership is local and diverse in background, but possibly splitting up in supporting different services.

For associational churches, membership is scattered and homogenous, so that differences of opinion lead to splits and withdrawals.

3. *Boundary between church and environment*

Communal church boundaries are blurred, with no clarity about who is in and who is out, because survival is not wholly dependent upon support from members. (Thus a member of a rural community in Essex, England, said: 'The church is the village and the village is the church'). In times of crisis support may come from unexpected sources (cf. the incident of Baldock church clock, p. 56).

Associational church boundaries are clearly drawn, because membership involves voluntary support and control of the institution, with responsibility for its survival.

4. *Value systems*

The communal church shares the values of its environment, and so tends to reinforce what is there. Members do not experience undue tension between values in church gatherings and values in their environment.

Associational churches promote value systems which are clearly different from the environment. Members are aware of the split and often feel they are in a losing battle with the less rigid values of their non-church environment.

5. *Institutional change*

The communal church, being aware of its historical roots in society, will tend to change by gradual reformation and adaptation from within.

Associational churches are more conscious of the eschatological dimensions of life (*ie* ultimate values), and they change by revolution or through the intervention of outside agencies and consultants, including therapists.

6. *Form of ministry*

Communal churches concentrate on the cyclic aspects of the oscillation process (*eg* festivals) and stress the corporate life of the church usually through sacramental life. (We are not restricting this to the so-called Catholic approach to the sacraments.)

Associational churches experience ups and downs. They organise special times for renewals and revivals, when the individual is the target more than the congregation as a whole.

7. *Emotional pattern of the activities*
   (cf. Appendix on Bion's theory)

In communal churches the dependent pattern will prevail, ranging from immature resourceless dependence to mature resourceful dependence. The present is always being judged by the past.

In associational churches the expectancy pattern will be dominant, where the hope for the future is in the young people or in the form of loving relationships among the worshippers, which it is hoped will make people feel at peace with themselves. These relations may be developed at the expense of outside existing ones. The present is continually being assessed by the future.

8. *Reaction to stress and conflict*

Communal churches accept that they are composed of ordinary people from the locality and realise there are good and bad elements mingled together. So they expect to live with the tension and disagreements and keep the fights internal (*ie* psychological splitting and projection on the outside world is at a minimum).

Associational churches need to see themselves as good objects to retain their membership, otherwise people will leave and go elsewhere. Therefore they deny their defects and project them on to the outside world. So the tension is external, between the church and the world. Internal splits cannot be tolerated and people including clergy leave abruptly.

9. *Method of joining the church*
Communal churches stress sacramental ways of becoming members: it is the role which changes.

Associational churches believe in the need for some form of conversion: it is the person who changes.

10. *Relation to the political structures (the State)*
The communal church has a symbiotic relationship which may be one of being established (*eg* Church of England), or being State-supported (*eg* Lutheran Church in Finland). It therefore tends to be conservative.

Associational churches are separate from the State. They may offer a substitute community with a full round of social activities, and consider themselves radical.

11. *Likely forms of dysfunctional religion*
Communal churches become shrines for folk religion because of their constant emphasis on the unchanging myths of the apostolic tradition. Since survival is contingent upon reliability, change is suspect, and this opens the way to a benign form of folk religion.

Associational churches need to be alert to changes in the environment and are always open to change, but the social interaction with the environment in the intra-dependent mode can lead to secularism and the collapse of the vitality of traditional religious symbolism. Alternatively the associational church may become so wrapped up in itself as a fantasy of a closed community that it is trapped in ecclesiasticism.

Some relations between communal churches and associational churches are worth noting. Where a communal church becomes monopolistic and does not allow for development within a given society then associational churches may form in protest, such as the Brownites (Congregationalists) in the time of Elizabeth I. If a monopolistic communal church fosters such an immature dependence that people cannot express the fight or expectancy sides of their personalities, then associational churches embodying these emotional patterns will emerge in compensation (*eg* for fight, the evangelical Methodists; for expectancy, the Quakers and their migration

to found Pennsylvania). Current expressions of the expectancy pattern may be observed in the charismatic movement
and the call for the ordination of women. Associational
churches can develop into communal churches; in parts of
South Yorkshire for example, Baptist chapels look like Anglican churches and are regarded as if they were so by many of
the population. A few sects become denominations which
spread out to cover whole areas and become communal
churches, such as the Mormons' Church of the Latter Day
Saints in the State of Utah. The amount of respect accorded
to leaders of local churches probably reflects whether they are
experienced as communal or associational churches; the
greater the respect, the more likely they lead communal
churches.

Two examples
  To conclude our description of these two types, we give
personal accounts illustrating dysfunctional tendencies in
churches of each type. The first shows how the folk religion
pattern can often be maintained with a good deal of sophistication:

> There is a strong community spirit in this village. There
> are old houses and an even more ancient church, lots of
> history and traditions from the past, and a determination
> to preserve the village's individual identity in the present.
> Geographically it is close to a big town, where most of the
> inhabitants of the village work, but the prevailing feeling is
> that we belong to the village. It is a concerned, friendly,
> caring village. Everyone who lives here meets a high stan-
> dard of good neighbourliness. The comment most fre-
> quently heard from newcomers is 'what a friendly place it
> is'.
>   I have lived here for three years, worshipping at the
> parish church and taking quite an active part in its life and
> activities. I find that the church both fosters the good
> neighbourly, friendly attitude of the village and is itself
> supported by it. In this respect there is outwardly very
> little difference in the behaviour of those who are members
> of the church and those who are not.

During this time I have been trying to work at the ideas as they have developed.[1] I managed to understand and accept intellectually the thesis of the paper, and could appreciate the truth of it at that level. But when it came to trying to apply it to my own situation I got completely stuck. Try as I might I could find nothing which seemed to apply to this village and parish. It was as if the ideas came from another world. I tried discussing them with other people in the church, but the more I tried the more stuck I got.

(I then heard) the comment ... made that sometimes a culture is so all-embracing that it smothers people, so that they cannot see what is happening in it ... Was *that* it? Was I so overwhelmed, swallowed and absorbed in this friendly, caring community culture (to which I am also a willing contributor) that I could not see it for what it was and therefore could not see the relevance of these ideas to it?

I had observed that the worship of the church was prepared with care and prayer, and conducted with dignity and reverence. Sermons, too, were Bible-based and thoughtful. But everything we did was all very comfortable, familiar and safe: sharper insights, which might be painful, were avoided or not uncovered. Only very rarely was there an evangelistic emphasis, and no-one seemed to expect or desire it. In short, the church seemed to be at pains not to 'rock the boat', not to emphasise that we as Christians might be expected in some way to be different and to do different things from other people. We seemed to be failing to acknowledge and look at those bits of the truth which could well be uncomfortable, if not downright divisive.

As a church we were concerned more with safety and with the self-preservation of the comfortable caring aspects of our community life than we were with the more daring truths of the christian Gospel. It seemed that we valued the priestly and pastoral roles of our church, but were failing to give the same kind of importance to its evangelistic responsibility. More especially, we had neglected the church's

---

[1] The ideas in this book, as presented in an earlier paper.

obligation to be prophetic – in the truly Biblical sense of declaring God's truth in the present, however much it brings us under His judgment.

A young curate describes how the associational 'daughter' church in the parish, for all its liveliness, had become absorbed in ecclesiasticism:

> Soon after arriving in the parish from theological college I had come to the conclusion that the parish church was dead and it was the daughter church where the Gospel was being preached effectively and taking root in people's lives. The parish church was 'middle of the road C of E' and very formal. The congregation had no wish to participate in leading the worship: they liked the clergy to take the whole service. When coffee was served in the hall after the service hardly anybody came. There were no midweek organisations. At the daughter church by contrast the laity took an active part in leading the services. There were over fifty leaders of children's groups and youth groups linked to the church, and the congregation had a strong sense of fellowship and a real enthusiasm for the work.
>
> As I began to think through these ideas about the role of the churches in society my view of both churches began to change. I came to recognise the way that people living in the town, particularly those who had lived there some time, saw the parish church as a stable centre of community life, standing for the enduring values of the old community. I stopped preaching sermons which held up the daughter church as a model of church life and compared the parish church unfavourably with it.
>
> The congregation at the daughter church includes a large number of families with young children, many of them fairly new to the area, relatively mobile people who will move away in a few years. Underneath the enthusiasm to share in the work in the church there often lies a search, sometimes a desperate search, to be accepted and to belong. This has made me feel that some people, in trying to meet this need, are spending an unhealthy amount of time in church activities, and my concern now is to work

out how I can enable them to find the strength through the church's worship to involve themselves in secular activities.

Chapter 8

The Leadership of the Local Church

The leadership of any institution is carried out formally by the allocation of persons to designated roles. The church is no exception and we wish to consider the various leadership roles in the local church bearing in mind the four types of activity systems (operating, managing, service and control), and whether the roles such as parish priest, rector, vicar, minister, elder, pastor, deacon, preacher, reader, as they are currently defined and carried out, are appropriate to these tasks. We are aware that these roles are mostly filled by men who are ordained or specially designated, and that non-ordained people, especially some women, feel that they have been unfairly excluded from some of these positions, although they are heavily involved in others.

There are several points we wish to make before proceeding further. The first is about leadership and management. For the sake of clarity, as distinct from being dogmatic, we will prefer the following definitions. *Management* is the regulation by a person or group of the boundaries between an institution and its external environment, between task activity systems and the internal environment of the institution, between the institution and its task activity systems, and between different task activity systems. *Leadership* is the capacity to attract followers in task performance. Both are functions of role (see below) but managers focus on the activity – they manage the process – while leaders concentrate on people – they lead followers. In what Fred Emery (1970) calls a 'socio-psychological system', where people are the throughput (in a 'socio-technical system' the throughputs are material not human), leadership is of special importance, but because churches are voluntary societies where the throughput themselves provide many human and material resources, leadership is of even more significance. Much organisational theory about churches fails to take these variables into account and falls into the mistake of treating churches like factories.

The second point follows on from leadership. The concept of *representation* is characteristic of all religious activity wherever someone represents God to other persons and those persons to God, as does the priest. In terms of the process we have shown how the churchgoers represent non-attenders and unbelievers in worship, the part representing and standing for the whole. In terms of the christian movement, Jesus represents God to humanity, and humanity to God; the Holy Spirit represents Jesus in the church, and the church represents Jesus to the world; while the poor, maimed and imprisoned represent Jesus to the church, and in prayer to God the worshipper represents those for whom he prays. It is comparatively easy for the believer to appreciate the corporateness of the church in understanding that the local church despite its frailty and errors represents the Body of Christ past, present and future, but it is much harder for the member of the Kingdom to perceive that he represents humanity to itself and to God in his daily life, because a person in a role, such as a factory manager, a nurse, a headmaster or a bishop, represents the system in which he works both to insiders and outsiders.

The third point is about terminology. By *laity* we mean the people who comprise the congregation of a local church, from whom certain persons are selected, those on whom each church corporately through its leaders consider the *kleros* or lot from God has fallen – the *clergy*, who declare this openly through their ordination. They are representatives therefore of God, and of the laity. We prefer our restricted use of laity, although we are aware that *laos* is now being generally applied to the whole people of God, because this wider meaning blurs the boundary between the two discrete functions of clergy and laity.

Fourthly we need to be clear about the concept *role* since many view the term with suspicion; thus a person is referred to as 'playing a role' when others feel he is game-playing or acting a part which is not a true expression of himself. If told they are allocated to a role, some people feel they are being forced into a mould and depersonalised. The concept can be approached from many standpoints. Apart from the theatre (role is derived from the French for the scroll which contains the actor's part), sociological approaches focus on roles in relation to society, and psychological approaches focus on roles in relation to persons. The former study the behaviour, the latter the experience of the person taking the role. We define role as:

> an idea which an individual holds in his mind according to which he organises his behaviour to perform certain activities (Reed, 1976).

A person who finds himself in a certain position, by choice, by command or involuntarily, employs his role-idea to regulate his behaviour to achieve a task in relation to the environment. In the course of his daily life a person fulfils many roles. One man may be husband, father, householder, engineer, voter, church secretary, Oxfam group organiser, football supporter, gardener. He has as many roles as the groups to which he belongs, or as the systems of activity in which he engages. In taking each role he selects attributes and skills from his capacities in order to do a particular job.

Each role activates a part of his person, and one might say that an individual is able to engage in as many roles as are needed to activate at one time or another the whole of his personality. His integrity then depends on whether he can relate each of these roles to one another and to himself as a whole person: how does he, for example, bring together his role as a sales manager with his role as church member. Role is experienced as limiting or restricting when people accept, thoughtlessly or under compulsion, someone else's role-idea and allow it to submerge their own. John Bunyan and Dietrich Bonhoeffer would not yield up their own roles as prophet and pastor when they were made prisoners. We suggest that role enables a person to concentrate a selection of his skills and abilities over a period of time for a particular purpose.

In defining role as an idea which an individual holds in his mind according to which he organises his behaviour, the assumption is made that W-activity is being described. However any group is simultaneously engaged in S-activity and insofar as the S-activity dominates the group's behaviour, its members fail to 'keep in role', the work role no longer controls their behaviour, and they are passively open to receive the projections of others' ideas about roles. Roles are locally assigned to different members of the group to try to ensure its survival under the stress they are now experiencing. One member may be held responsible and blamed for the inadequacies of the group and thus be assigned the role of scapegoat. In this sense we speak of *assigned role* as distinct from *work role*. We will concentrate on work roles allocated for the performance of a task in the church and provide an analysis which delineates the attitudes and behaviour of those holding the role-idea and compare it with the expectations of others.

Fifthly and finally we need to comment on the thorny problem of authority. We will use *authority* to mean that attribute of a role which gives a person access to resources to enable him to carry out his assigned task. A judge, for example, has authority to pronounce sentence on a convicted criminal, because he can direct others, the police and the prison service, to see that his verdict is acted on. This definition can be sharpened up by setting it alongside the concept *power*, by which we mean the attributes of a person or persons which enable them to do things. There are different types of power – that which comes from personal qualities, skills or experience so one can do things oneself; that which comes from possession of objects such as a gun, money or slaves; that which is conferred on someone by others' respect or dependence such as the power given to a charismatic leader; and that which a person can seize because of his status or office, by misusing resources for personal reasons rather than for the designated task, commonly called authoritarianism. For example the London policeman by virtue of his role has authority to secure a warrant to enter a house to arrest persons suspected of a crime. His power comes from his skill and physique and, less often than in the past, from his well-known uniform which leads the public to support him. But because he is not armed he may be tempted to exploit his status for personal gain, which may then lead him into corruption.

A priest of the Church of England is ordained into a role for which he is given the authority to preach the Word and minister the sacraments. When instituted into a parish he receives authority for the 'cure of souls' in the parish with the right to use the resources of the parish church. But before his ordination and his induction it is the duty of those responsible to see he has the requisite power in terms of personal qualities including spirituality and skills, and also leadership. Otherwise, lacking these powers he may fall back on his position to assert himself.

We will tackle the subject of leadership roles in the church in two parts; first by exploring roles in the *operating system* of activities which carry out the primary task of the local church, and including the service system; and in the following chapter by examining roles in the *managing system*, referring also to the control system where appropriate.

Roles can be related to the various stages in the oscillation process as shown in Diagram 3 (and cf. Weber, 1922, chs. 2, 4, 5 especially). We shall discuss each of these four roles in turn.

The Priest/Presbyter

The role of the priest is:

> to ensure the performance of the primary task of the local church by setting up activities which contain or render manageable the anxieties associated with the profane world (p. 148).

He does this through the following three sub-tasks:

> (a) to assist worshippers and prospective worshippers to manage their regression to extra-dependence;
> (b) to provide opportunities for them to worship God;
> (c) to provide opportunities for them to make the transition from extra-dependence to intra-dependence.

Diagram 3

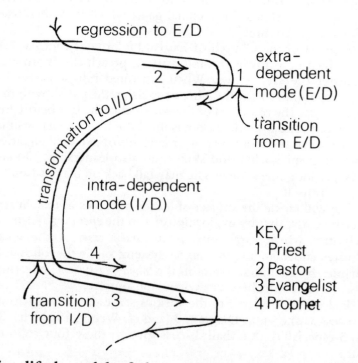

Simplified model of the oscillation process showing leadership roles in the church institution

To do these tasks he has not only a wide variety of resources (p. 119) but also access to the voluntary help and resources of the laity.

The paramount skill of the priest (or the presbyter) is to be aware of and sensitive to process whether consciously or unconsciously. He can then sympathise with the weak and rejoice in the strength of the free. He will know the power of ritual to evoke symbols and discharge feelings, and be able to lead it so that worshippers can be without distractions in worshipping God. Above all else he needs to appreciate the place of dependence in life and to be able to work with people in the dependent condition.

Without these basic skills and insights he will only misuse the treasures of the christian movement. With them, he can appreciate and set forth the symbolic language and actions of the apostolic faith for the support, guidance and enrichment of the worshippers. He is able by his own conscious and deliberate investment in this S-activity to manage his own behaviour, so that liturgy becomes a 'service', an offering, to God and to the worshippers. The false priest is one who serves himself, either deliberately or because he is so unskilled that he has to utilise the occasion to cope with his own anxieties.

The priest, when he conducts the liturgy, is in a perpetual tension because in order to manage the S-activity for the benefit of the worshippers, including himself, he has to maintain W-activity. The alternative is either to be caught up in ecstatic utterances, wild gestures and unco-ordinated movement or to be remote, cold-blooded and manipulative, which justifies Jean Anouilh's statement that 'a religious phenomenon is a ceremony of lying'. Because of this immense strain the priest needs to be clear about his boundaries, so that he knows exactly what to do and say, and be confident in what he represents. The development of set liturgies aids both these, by taking away the uncertainty about content and diminishing anxiety about W-activity, and the ancient historic origins of elements of the liturgy strengthen his identity as a representative of the truth and wisdom which is derived from the apostles. The use of robes and vestments shows the distinctive role he is taking, and the architecture of the building and arrangement of furniture give clear signals about the significance of the successive phases of liturgy.

During the service and after, the priest needs to be on the alert to his own human reactions. If he tends towards over-scrupulousness in concentrating on too many details which makes the ritual wooden or disjointed, he realises that he is using the ceremony as a defence of himself against his anxieties and fears. He has gone out of role and been overwhelmed by S-activity. If he throws his prayer book away and behaves spontaneously he may be experiencing the overruling of the Holy Spirit, or he may be succumbing to the seduction of the congregation's regression to extra-dependence which he is unable to control.

If he is experiencing more love, power or hate than he feels is reasonable, given the realities he is aware of, then he can predict the worshipping congregation are using him as an object on which to project parts of themselves. From the outset he expected that in his role as priest the congregation would use him like this, but he could be unsure as to the precise way they would use him. The congregation may want to project on him the parts of themselves they value as important, so he will feel powerful, admired and probably effective. With insight he appreciates they are having difficulty in controlling their regression on God, and therefore using him as a substitute receptacle. His only proper response may be to endure this projection without being misled into pretentiousness and vanity about himself, so that the congregation seeing his lack of regard for their manipulation, for such it is, will be assisted to renew their search for the conception of God. In this way he jolts them out of helplessness, from resourceless dependence, a state where passively they sit back and expect him to work miracles for them. In refusing to be manipulated he knows that the congregation, or some members of it, may become angry at what they consider his lack of concern for them, and turn on him; in psychological terms, they withdraw their good parts and instantly replace them with the parts of themselves about which they are guilty and afraid – the bad parts. So quickly do we topple favourites and crucify saviours. The key to the christian priest's behaviour is his confidence in the efficacy of the myths and symbols of the movement he represents. The essential dynamic he stands for is that contemplation of the conception of the God disclosed by Jesus enables worshippers to become peaceful within themselves and feel powerful enough to face the unknown hazards of life and death. To convey this efficacy to the worshipping believers he celebrates the redemptive acts of Jesus in the Holy Communion. His task there is to enable the worshippers to present their inner worlds to God in all their confusion, sin and weakness, and then to take back into themselves those parts they have projected on to God and reconstitute them within themselves; in symbolic terms each believer presents his sin to Christ 'who bore our sins in his body on the tree' (I Peter 2:24) and identifies himself with Christ in his death, being 'buried with him so that ... (he) might be raised to new life with him' (Romans 6:4).

Secondly, if the priest's feeling of depression is out of all proportion to his own circumstances he may be experiencing some projections and recognise that the worshippers have brought in from the environment their fears and impotence about their economic, social and political conditions, a circumstance which may be common to all the congregation or concentrated in a few prominent church members. His problem here is that instead of controlled regression there are signs of containment and withdrawal, and omens of hopelessness. There is no sense in trying to rally the worshippers with hearty hymns or exploit their condition by preaching judgment. All the priest can do is to receive the depression into himself, be 'touched with their infirmities', and set up a personal inner dialectic with his own faith, in the hope that he may generate a counter force which can spread through the congregation, and release them to engage in controlled regression where their fears and impotence can be relieved of their terror, and they can receive confidence to cope with the realities they represent.

A third possibility is where the priest finds himself flooded with excitement and expectations. Perhaps he has the impulse to hurry through the service so that the congregation can discuss the future of the church, possibly because it has outgrown the buildings. Sober reflection may lead him to consider that behind the realistic need for future planning was the devaluation of the actual conduct of, and participation in, the liturgy. If the congregation consists of many parents with young children, or the church is on a new development estate, or the congregation has had an influx of new members, he may reach the conclusion that in order to avoid facing issues about present dependence the congregation has resorted to flight into hope about the future. The old is dead, long live the new. The acute tension for the priest is to share their hopes and allow them to use him to preserve their hopes and anxieties about the future, but be anchored to the liturgy and take the risk of being stranded as the tide goes out. Some local churches split the role here, and the assistant curate or minister carries the hope leaving the incumbent to sustain the dependence. Where there is only one priest he will have a hard struggle to be a symbol of the need for regression and dependence by being dependable himself, and not become only a banker to preserve their hopes.

These are three examples of a priest being faced with issues arising from dependence. Our hypothesis is that his role is designed to attract them in order that they can be dealt with constructively. There is nothing pathologically wrong with most congregations. Functional religious behaviour is not 'intuitive'; otherwise there would be no need for movement, only for process. In the course of learning to worship God, much dysfunctional behaviour can be anticipated. Feelings of sin, guilt, judgment are signs of healthy behaviour. Only a healthy person can be held accountable for his sin; or can handle his guilt before God. Therefore priests are not therapists but teachers.

But priests are under great pressure to conform to a different model of the role. In Britain and other parts of the Anglo-Saxon culture including the United States, to be dependent is undesirable, and a person who advocates it is often deemed to be an immature child or a sick adult. The associated concepts of sin, guilt and so on are likewise branded unhealthy, and consequently worshippers cannot be held accountable for sin, because today people are not normally held responsible for their illnesses, and therefore are not in need of forgiveness from God. Instead they go into therapy and experience dependence on their analyst, having been deprived by what we would consider bad interpretations of human behaviour of the relief from depression to be obtained from christian forgiveness and regeneration. Consequently the priest role has been eroded and been replaced by those of therapists, counsellors, social workers and experts in behavioural studies.

A role is not a solid entity like a diamond but a fluctuating and constantly renewed idea like a candle flame. We have identified factors like process, dependence and symbolic language as basic ingredients of the role, and so when we observe behaviour which denies their crucial place we become uneasy about the motive. Some priests who are under pressure from their colleagues to repudiate the centrality of dependence are bound to feel bewildered about who they are. This confusion is compounded because innovative ideas which objectively have much to commend them can be linked up with the denial of dependence. Lay participation in the liturgy is one such idea, but a member of a church where laity are fully involved in planning and running the services said that his congregation did not believe in dependence but in sharing, and though it was obvious that there was considerable extra-dependence on the priest, attempts were always being made to interpret the Gospel in terms of human relationships.

The considerable technical content of the role is an important factor in the current discussions advocating the diminution of the difference between the roles of priest and laity. We consider that to carry out the priest role is for most people not a voluntary activity because of the strain and stress the priest needs to work with in fulfilling it. It is not a matter of being trained and then taking the role from time to time, but one which requires continual analysis, and ongoing involvement with the local community, which a person who goes out to work elsewhere cannot do. How much of the role of priest can safely be delegated to laity is a decision which is contingent on the circumstances and the people involved. The ordained clergy therefore remain for us the most appropriate persons to take the corporate role of the priesthood of all believers.

Earlier we have shown how local churches can proliferate weekday activities to compensate for their inability to make the transition to intra-dependence, and named it ecclesiasticism. When clergy lose touch with their priestly role the boundary between what is activity appropriate to the role and what is not appropriate becomes blurred, so they may succumb to pressures from laity to create a busy weeklong programme in order to avoid the failed act in worship. This is no blanket condemnation of church programmes. We are trying to enunciate a principle and each must be judged on its merits.

If we have made our point, this analysis raises huge questions about the preparation and *formation* of priests, especially when it is remembered that ordained clergy usually have additional roles including that of pastor. Priests need to be persons who know the world in which they live, and know themselves, a mature undertaking which is why the New Testament churches spoke of elders (presbyters). Indications about the formation are scattered throughout this book, but the real work on this subject has yet to be done.

What we have said about the actual service of worship can readily be expanded to cover the other aspects of the role. Baptism involves working with projections particularly because many parents who request baptism for their children may not be accustomed to meeting priests. The same applies to weddings and funerals. If the priest ministers to a local church of the communal type (p. 157) then he and the church building will attract those whose religious behaviour is of the dysfunctional religious type classified as folk religion and who express it through christian symbols. That priest has two co-incident roles – he is priest/presbyter of the apostolic religion and at the same time the local cult priest of the community folk religion. He may repudiate the role when approached personally, but unless he turns his church into one of the associational type, the community will continue to regard him as such. Given an understanding of the interaction between process and movement, a priest skilled in working with dependence could minister to folk religionists with some possibility that he is able to meet and satisfy their religious needs without being unfaithful to his apostolic role. In churches where there is confession or the rite of penance the priest is specifically concerned with regression to extra-dependence. If he is able to use symbolism sensitively and deal with the dependency problems of the confessional he may be able to guide the penitent into functional religious behaviour. However when the Roman Catholic Church relaxed its discipline over confession such a large proportion ceased going to confession weekly that its contribution to apostolic religion is suspect. It was more a sign of the power of the priest than of his authority.

We consider the other Occasional Offices (as these services of Matrimony, Burial of the Dead, etc. are sometimes called) are very important aspects of the priest role because they enable him to demonstrate that the local church is a part of the whole community.

We have already discussed preaching and teaching. Teaching is an essential part of the priest role which entails the presentation and transmission of the traditional symbols and myths that constitute the christian movement and interpreting them for contemporary cultural conditions. In his ordination the priest is given 'authority to preach the Word of God . . . in the congregation'. He will not however be able to exercise that authority unless he can be clear about the primary task of the church congregation to which he is appointed. If the preacher sees his function only as communication of ideas between pulpit and pew and does not, at least in his mind, relate it to the primary task then he may be speaking great truths which God will honour, but he will not be advancing apostolic religion because he is displaying his personal power more than his authority.

The priest has a lonely job. If he is consistently aware of his dependent relationships, he will learn things about himself and others which cannot be shared with anyone else in the local church. He experiences some of the aloneness of Christ on the cross. Group ministries which try and mitigate this loneliness may give some personal satisfaction to the priest at the expense of depriving the local church of a clearly designated leader which they require if they are to deal with their dependent condition in a functional way. It would be infinitely preferable for each priest to have an adviser or confessor outside the locality, but of course this task is really intrinsic to the role of the Bishop or the equivalent overseeing minister in other churches.

The following account by a Roman Catholic priest conveys his experience of the loneliness of his role and how he has come to terms with it:

As a Roman Catholic priest I work in a large city parish which on the surface has a lively and successful liturgy.

There are six Masses every Sunday, and an overall atten- dance of nearly 2,000. But still I sometimes feel uneasy. Most of the people who come to Mass are very indi- vidualistic. They want to get on with their own devotions in private and resist most efforts to make them participate actively or be even conscious of one another. I long for them to get hold of a vision of the Church as the People of God, and experience the Sunday Mass as the gathering of the local community of believers.

There is always a crowd standing at the back. Once I coaxed them to come forward by complaining how difficult it is for the priest facing all those empty rows in the front. They came forward then, sheepishly, embarras- sed – but next week they were back in their usual place.

Sometimes as I stand at the altar I feel the concentrated gaze of the congregation almost too much, making me into something I do not feel myself to be. They do not want me too close to them. They want me to be different, and that makes me feel separated and distanced, when part of me would prefer to be among them as one of them.

My approach to the liturgy has theological justification, but it also reflects my own needs. I can see that part of the reason I blackmailed people to come forward to the front rows arose out of my own feelings of isolation. My con- cern to make people conscious of one another reflects my own loneliness and search for community. People's desire that I should be different and separate from them reflects their need for a dependent leader, so that the isolation I feel is a proper part of the burden of the priesthood.

It has made me realise more clearly the difference be- tween my liturgical role and my pastoral role. Closeness to the people is developed outside the liturgy, and I have consciously tried to work at this: visiting more, welcom- ing people to the presbytery, chatting before and after Mass. I find it frees me from the need to experience per- sonal closeness during the liturgy itself. I can accept the distance and feel less personally threatened by it. I do not mind their using me for their own needs in worship.

In his aloneness the priest can contemplate the corporateness of the local church he serves. Does the symbolic activity evoke fantasies which bring the congregation into a sense of wholeness, at the same time enabling its membership to feel integrated with the surrounding locality and responsible for it? If his answer is in the affirmative then he can expect that the values of that social and political environment will be brought into the church for testing in the presence of God, and the symbols of the church will have a powerful effect on the imagination and creativity of the population generally. Even if haltingly and stutteringly, that church is carrying out its primary task.

As can be seen we have concentrated our effort on the communal type of church because it is easier to relate to the oscillation process. Associational type churches have a much more complex problem because singly they cannot identify with the surrounding society without appearing presumptuous. Their act of compensation is therefore to swallow as much of the environment as possible and mastermind a mini-community centred on the church. In this type of institution the priest has a role just as we have described but though his leadership is important and he is subject to the projections relating to regression to extra-dependence the behaviour may be covert and difficult to work with, because at the overt level the church itself only survives as long as it remains a good object for its members. Instead therefore of positive projections on the priest as God's emissary and the congregation working with their own negative and bad feelings within themselves, they are likely to retain their good feelings and project their bad feelings *outside* the church on to the world, rendering the priest role more or less impotent.

These generalisations may be compared with this account by a Methodist minister:

I became aware of the character of the church's worship in my first few months as a new minister in the circuit. It was full of warmth, enjoyment and a sense of goodness. The building was warm and comfortable, with a modernised interior. Hymns were sung with enthusiastic loyalty; as the preacher I had the constant attention of the congregation. But after a time something in the mood of the services disturbed me. It felt too good, too nice, and I had a sense of constraint as to what I could and could not say in the services.

One idea[1] ... stuck in my mind: do the worshippers consider the real life situations from which they have come, or does their worship provide a way of escape from these realities or a method of justifying a simplistic view of them? On looking back I realised that in this church, unlike other churches in the circuit, I kept on omitting prayers of confession and forgiveness from the order of service. This seemed to tie in with my feeling that although the congregation gave their attention to the sermon they did not want to be engaged emotionally with any exploration of badness in men or of sinfulness before God. I remembered that the stewards had told me of the complaints they had registered with the Superintendent about local preachers who preached about sin, death, judgment and hell. I found myself thrown back into a painful period of self-examination and soul-searching.

I struggled to make my own worship true to my experience of life, and in my sermons to speak of life as I knew I and others experienced it. I began to include a prayer of confession and a declaration of forgiveness in each service, and preached sermons attempting to encourage the congregation to enter into worship by way of confession. How far this has been effective I find very hard to judge, but subsequently members of the congregation have spoken more freely to me about their problems in the course of pastoral visits and conversations.

Another feature of this tendency to preserve the church as a 'good' place from which all 'badness' was excluded was the idealisation of certain members of the church, particularly a family who had been leaders in the church, as stewards, trustees and Sunday School teachers, for nearly fifty years. Through pastoral work when one of the family died, I was allowed to participate in the inner life of the family, and to hear of the conflicts within it, of their feelings about several of their children who had left the area

[1] An idea in a previous draft of this book.

and broken off their links with any church, and of the pain they felt over the change of the local community from a country village to a sprawling suburb. This opportunity to explore the negative and painful aspects of their lives with me seemed to release them to respond more positively to the changes taking place in the community.

The Pastor

The role of pastor augments that of priest in working at the primary task of the local church. Since most clergy combine the two roles they tend to become blurred; though there is some overlap, they cover separate activities. The specific sub-task of the pastoral role is:

> to assist people to regress to extra-dependence and transform to intra-dependence through personal ministry.

Whereas the priest role of clergy relates the ministry to the sacred space more or less within the extra-dependent mode, the pastor works at the interface between the sacred and profane world by meeting people where they are. The priest sees the local church as a corporate whole, the pastor sees it as a collective group of families and individuals, a flock, for whose lost sheep he cares. The work of the pastor shows whether his church is of the associational type or the communal type, depending upon whom he considers his responsibility – if only church members and those who have declared an interest in the church, then an associational type; if he regards everyone as a parishioner, then a communal type.

The role may be carried out through visiting and hospitality when advising, counselling and teaching takes place. Depending upon their interpretation of the task, pastors will operate quite differently. The contrast between the clergy of two denominations in the same town illustrates this. Clergy from one denomination were unable to extricate themselves from a relation with their parishioners where visiting was seen as a social call, when it became awkward to speak of the church in any realistic way. They found themselves chatting with a wife whose husband they wanted to see while trying to balance a cup of tea in one hand and a sandwich in the

other, so that they could not concentrate effectively on anything. Clergy from the other denomination saw it much
more clearly as a working visit. They went to the back door
if possible, poked their head in and asked if all was well or if
they were needed in any way, and unless there was a particular reason for staying soon left to visit another home. The
first group of clergy were obviously unclear about their role
and hence their authority was lacking; the others were clear
and were heard as having authority. The former group lost
their pastoral role and became fixed in social roles. Instead of
a dependence condition being maintained, this was suppressed and replaced by an overt expectancy condition which
made it difficult to get up and leave. In other words, unless
the pastor in his visiting can draw a task boundary for the
visit he has no context in which to engage in symbolic activity in either phase of regression or transformation. The
opportunities are there but unusable, as in the case of the
young Methodist minister who could not understand why he
was treated with such deference by people in their homes,
until he realised that his very presence caused them to begin
to regress to extra-dependence.

Sick visiting, hospital and institutional visiting open doors
to pastoral work as do occasions surrounding birth, death
and marriage. In these cases the overlap between priest and
pastor is evident and, by celebrating Holy Communion, for
example, the priest can immediately create a sacred space.

The problem is that there are few models for pastoral work
which are now universally recognised by laity. Once it was
prayer and Bible reading but not now, even if that were desirable. Contemporary models often rely on evoking the
awareness of aspects of the oscillation process through discussion about personal, family or business life, rather than
rehearsing the symbols of the movement. Because of the
frequently unsatisfactory experiences of visiting, pastors
invite people to set up tasks for themselves and ask for counselling. This ostensibly becomes a work assignment and may
be an effective discussion in intra-dependence terms but have
little to do with the church's task in extra-dependence.

Thus the pastor role tends to drift. And if that pastor is also
conscious as priest of twisted issues about dependence then he

may encourage the drift into the intra-dependent mode, so under the guise of pastor he becomes an educationalist, a marriage guidance counsellor or a social worker. On the other hand, if he has strong views about the need for regeneration he may take up the role of prophet by giving his views of the relation between the work of the church and the condition of society.

The skill of the pastor is in his sensitivity to the human predicament of those he meets, and in his capacity to summon up a response which assists the person even a very little to live with his predicament. One part of the predicament often is that the person does not know how to regress to extra-dependence. Any symbols they knew which could have assisted in the transition from intra-dependence may have been drained of their power through intellectualising, or due to a bad experience years before the thought of dependence may now be humiliating. This state could occur when pain associated with a bad event, such as the death of a member of the family in a car accident, which evokes the need for a primal object (who is expected to perform miracles because the regression is uncontrolled), is transferred to the condition of dependence itself because that envisioned relationship was so unsatisfactory. The pastor needs to know about the oscillation process model or some similar model to untangle this knot, and enable the person to build the experience back into his life, and show he can manage his regression to extra-dependence.

It is often suggested that the pastoral role could be taken by laity. Undoubtedly there are laity who have social skills, a knowledge of life and sufficient knowledge of the christian life and message to be acceptable to the clergy as associates. The snag is that while as persons they may be made welcome, neither the people who really need spiritual help nor the outsider to church affairs regards them as proper representatives of 'the church'. Like the young Methodist minister, we easily underrate the symbolic presence of a clergyman in clerical dress. Known members of the church are not usually affected by this problem. The group who needed help may get it more readily because the lay member called, so that becomes a way of sorting out priorities. But the group who have a folk religious attitude could be affronted very easily, making a bigger problem for the communal type church than for the associational type.

Differences between the pastor role in associational and communal churches are slight, except where a new contact is invited to church. The associational church pastor makes him feel welcome, but he fears the strings attached; the communal church pastor makes him feel guilty because he has not been going (an indicator of vicarious oscillation) and he has difficulty getting over that hurdle.

The Evangelist

The role of the evangelist is to facilitate the primary task of the church by introducing the symbolic language of the christian movement to those without it, or with distorted versions of it. His sub-task can be defined as:

> to make available the symbolic language of the christian movement as an interpretation of the oscillation process.

Since the lack of potent symbols inhibits individuals from making a functional transition from intra-dependence, his work is of particular importance at that point in the oscillation process.

Both priest and evangelist appreciate the importance of myth and symbol but they see it from different positions. The priest begins with the fantasies evoked by the S-activity of the process, while the evangelist concentrates on the symbols of the movement. The priest may therefore tend towards undervaluing the movement in performing his rites and ceremonies; while the evangelist may become impatient and feel the 'superstitions' of the rituals interfere with the 'truth' of the Gospel (though the modern evangelist has plenty of his own rituals, as anyone who has been to a Billy Graham Crusade will testify). The evangelist has to spell out the details of the regression phase in order to guide those who respond to his symbolism.

By definition the movement comes from outside the culture which has evolved the process, and because the evangelist embodies the christian movement he is probably more effective as an outsider. In many local churches the essential thing is to get someone who is a stranger to lead a mission, which may be the reason why many evangelists become inveterate travellers.

If the evangelist is a stranger to the culture then some conflict is likely to arise from his message, as we have seen earlier with Paul the Apostle. The introduction of new symbols will challenge the old ones, and disrupt the values of the society because religious symbols arising in another culture will inevitably import the values of that culture since they have shaped the symbols' original form. Evangelism if successful may dislocate the existing relations of a social group with its environment and impose on it new cultural forms which may not be able to be absorbed into the existing culture which will be suppressed. Missionaries dressed black boys in 'short' pants not because it was appropriate for the Africans but because it was their own custom.

Indeed the missionary movement originating from the Western world provides a good example of this cultural clash. What many missionaries were slow to realise was that their prospective converts were often more interested in some of the imported values, political, commercial, technological and cultural, than they were in the religious symbols. Dr Stanley persuaded the Ugandans to receive missionaries so they could hear the Gospel, but when they arrived the Ugandans were dismayed because they had no guns which they needed to fight their enemies. They had been convinced by Stanley's guns, not by his words. Unfortunately many missionaries did not stay long enough to work through this clash of cultures, as it were to incarnate the symbolic language in the myths of the evangelised tribes.

By temperament evangelists may therefore be classed as fighters and flighters, and often they have few scruples in turning the Gospel into slogans – 'Ye must be born again'. Local churches which focus attention on evangelism instead of grappling with the issues of dependence in depth take this for granted. For them the need is to arm the 'christian soldiers' for the fight, and worship as we have expounded it is neglected.

In contrast with priest and pastor, the role of evangelist is open to clergy or laity, men and women alike, the basic requirement being the ability to speak clearly about faith in Jesus Christ as Lord. The more informed he is about Scripture and the teaching of the church or churches with whom he works, the greater the possibility of gearing his work in with them. The boundaries of the role need not be so drawn that the work is limited to formal occasions in church, in halls or in the market place, when people take up the role in public. The evangelist with imagination and initiative can find opportunities at all times. But there are caution signs to observe.

Because the evangelist considers he has authority from God to preach the Gospel, he feels free of sanctions which apply to other people. So John Wesley could maintain 'The world is my parish', to the discomfort of Anglican clergy in whose parishes he set up his societies. They did not see his authority but they were threatened by his power. The evangelist therefore needs to be clear about his task, and thus be precise about the boundaries within which he operates, recognising that he needs to have freedom in order to work, since he scatters the seed of the Word more like the primitive farmer than the modern counterpart who drills them precisely in rows. The role of evangelist is however not confined to persons preaching or teaching. It can be extended to cover any event or object which displays the symbols of the christian movement and at any time. The church building with its stained glass, cross or crucifix is one, the sight of a christian praying is a second, literature, music, paintings and sculpture are others. By presenting the apostolic symbols in beautiful and striking ways, they begin to provide shapes for the fantasies of the people who see and experience them. If they are memorable to an individual, at a time when he searches for help in facing some regression experience, these symbols are brought to mind and become active in re-presenting the fantasies which facilitate the transition to regression, by supporting and giving meaning to his anxieties and hopes.

Our proposition is that the evangelist is effective where he can offer his services at the point of transition from intra-dependence to regression. In suggesting this we have taken a role derived from the movement and located it within the process. The apparent success of evangelism on late night broadcasting is an interesting pointer as a way of getting a hearing from a person after a day's work, wanting to relax but not knowing how to do so. If evangelism is to promote functional religion the evangelist needs to work in close harmony with the priest who can brief him about the local culture, guide him about where to apply his preaching, and ensure that it contributes to the primary task of the church.

Because the roles of evangelist, and that which follows, prophet, are service functions to the churches generally, their work cannot be considered in relation to one single local church, because unlike the priest and pastor they do not work in relation to the church as a local institution but as a collective of churches within wider cultures. Though we have interpreted these two roles within this wider environment the issues raised are capable of application at local church level.

The Prophet

The first three terms were at least in general use in the local church, but 'prophet' may appear archaic and irrelevant. What happened was that in pursuing our study of the oscillation hypothesis a role emerged which matched with that of prophet.

The task of the prophet is to evaluate the performance by the church of its primary task. He does not judge its effectiveness by its attendance, spirituality or the scope of its activities, which are the measures so often used by the members of the churches themselves. His yardstick is the state of the society in which the church works. Does that society exhibit the marks of righteousness, justice, peace and freedom for all its inhabitants or not? If not, then the religious practices of the nation are vain, worthless and misleading. Amos remarks on the futility of sacrifices (5:22), Jeremiah on the waste of time spent in relying on the Temple (7:4).

The prophet declares that God's concern is for the nation, and so he addresses the whole society even if he is only speaking to a part. His attitude forcibly reminds us that church members in another role belong to that society. Any criticism therefore is addressed to them alongside all their fellow citizens, and there is no escape or mitigation for anyone. While some prophets in the Old Testament castigated certain people specifically (Amos 7:16f), the nation is not divided into sheep or goats, all are in the same boat under God's judgment or under his blessing. A serious mistake by the churches is to blame society or groups within that society. For example in Northern Ireland leaders of the different churches blamed the paramilitary groups and accused them of the evils they were all suffering; the prophetic stance is to judge the Province for allowing these things to happen and confess the failure of the churches in not being able to prevent it, accepting that the churches are under the same condemnation as anyone else. We consider that because of the critical part of religion in the troubles, the inability of the churches to speak with such a prophetic voice may have been a cause in prolonging the strife.

The role of the prophet therefore puts the churches in their place. The task of the church is to serve the purpose God has for humanity, not to be concerned for itself. It is God's instrument for good, and it neglects its mission if it becomes obsessed with its own behaviour. God does love and care for his church because he has founded it, but that does not give the churches the right to say that they have a monopoly over him; God does not belong to the churches.

The agony of the prophet is that he feels he will not achieve his end. Jeremiah felt this deeply:

'Woe is me, my mother, that you bore me, a man of strife and contention to the whole land! I have not lent, nor have I borrowed, yet all of them curse me' (Jeremiah 15:10).

Two things sustain the prophet. First, that he has a strong conviction that he speaks on God's behalf and that God's word is in his mouth (Jeremiah 1:9f; Ezekiel 2:8–3:33), enabling him to see the totality and not be partial in what he declares. Second, that he identifies himself with the people to whom he speaks, and shares their suffering. Out of his inner struggles with his pain the prophetic 'burden' or 'vision' emerges. Only on the basis of his participation in their misfortunes does he have the right to speak of God's judgment on them, because it is also on himself. He may or may not be a 'paid up member' of the church, the focus is on the wider issue – God and nations.

We speak of nations rather than society in general because prophets of the Old Testament were sent to speak to kings and leaders of states. They were fit persons to be addressed as they stood for their nation, a concept of corporateness we have lost since Shakespeare could refer to Elizabeth and mean England, and the prayer for the King's Majesty in the 1549 Book of Common Prayer could mean that in praying for the King one prayed for oneself and all other of his subjects. The prophet deals with authority and power because that is the way changes are brought about which affect the state of the nation. There is nothing voluntary about this. In declaring judgment the prophet does not say 'please'. The strange mixture of anger and grudging admiration towards revolutionary groups and guerilla bands in their frontal attacks on governments, shows that there may be something of the prophet in them. But they speak of themselves executing judgment, not of God, as do the prophets of which we speak.

The message of the prophet is invariably one of judgment. He is a fail-safe mechanism triggered off when religion in a society is failing. The consistent theme of all the prophets is that the nation must turn to God or its sentence will be made even more severe. The effect desired by the prophets is to induce regression to extra-dependence, but his attack on them is while they are firmly in intra-dependence.

It is because he believes he has the authority to speak to the leaders of the country that the prophet has the right to break in on a people pre-occupied with running that country, making a living and enjoying themselves. He does not care that they are in intra-dependence; according to him they should be on their knees in extra-dependence. No wonder God said to Jeremiah:

See, I have set you this day over nations, and over kingdoms, to pluck up and to break down and destroy and to overthrow, to plant and to build (Jeremiah 1:10).

In broad strokes and bright colours the prophets paint cartoons of the New Jerusalem which will follow the repentance and regeneration of the nation. Their ideal state could never exist on earth, but it provides us with fantasy symbols which can energise and strengthen those citizens of earthly states in their daily life who consider they already are invisible members of the Kingdom of God through their own regeneration into it.

We have endeavoured to make clear that the role of prophet is distinct from the role of evangelist. The evangelist looks toward the church for his conception of God, the prophet toward the nations of the world. We doubt whether prophets would speak to churches, though priests seem always to be around prophets. Perhaps it is because the priests carry on where the prophet leaves off – in the sense today, that the church has to enable the nation to manage its regression to extra-dependence if it does repent.

Prophets are not produced to order by nation or church. We suspect that if there is a prophet around today he/she is working out an apprenticeship in an obscure place where he can engage with people at the depths of their experiences. Maybe raising the consciousness of oppressed groups of a society until they become a class of protestors against injustice in the name of the people and God, but maybe just waiting for that moment when he will be called before Prime Ministers, General Secretaries of Trade Unions, Presidents and Senate Committees. Once there, let him beware. They will be surrounded by false prophets, concerned only for their own class, crying 'Peace, Peace' – while God keeps saying 'There is no peace for the wicked'.

Other roles

There are many more roles and systems in the local church than those we have described. (Some, like those of Church Councils, are reserved for our discussion on Managing Systems in Chapter 9.) Some are auxiliary roles to that of priest and pastor, a few of which are: assistant clergy, church wardens, elders, sidesmen, acolytes, organist and choir, altar guild, service planning committee, pastoral committee, all of which directly support the priest and pastor roles.

A second cluster of service systems can be identified as those which provide some opportunity for their members to learn more about the christian faith or to apply it in the service of others. The list is immense but typical examples are: Sunday schools, prayer groups, mission committees, Bible study groups, discussion groups, healing groups, young people's evangelistic groups and fellowships, Christian study centres.

A third cluster comprises those which have a religious basis but include the overt object of socialising. Once again we can give only representative examples: Mothers' Union, wives' groups, men's groups, couples' groups, girls' and boys' uniformed organisations.

A fourth cluster consist of events designed mainly for recreation, general interest and social occasions: parties, dances, whist drives, gymnasiums, sports teams, Scouts and Guides, nursery schools.

We recognise that for some churches these activities are more important than worship services which are no more than 'the tip of the iceberg' as we have been told. We have questioned the purpose of those in the second, third and fourth clusters, believing that they are more the effects of dysfunctional religious behaviour than evidence of new spiritual insights. We tend to think of some of them as Martha groups, *ie* as having worthy motives but full of activity in contrast to Mary sitting quietly at the feet of Jesus – a clear picture of extra-dependence (Luke 10:38–42). Other groups and organisations, particularly in the third and fourth clusters are designed to build up a community life centred on the church, rather like a community centre or a country club, which causes us to call them friendship groups.

Considering that both Martha groups and friendship groups have greatly increased at a time when the influence of the churches in the national life are on the wane (we speak particularly of Britain), and given the implantation of other cultures leading towards a pluralistic society, this may be evidence that the primary task of the church is changing, of which we will have more to say in a final postscript.

But if our present hypothesis is correct, it may be worth

reconsidering whether all these extra activities are not draining away the skills which could be invested in services of worship, and tying up capital which might be used on keeping more churches open for services.

Chapter 9

The Managing System of the Local Church

Managing systems involve taking account of interaction between an enterprise and its environments. In studying the local church we have taken account of its environment insofar as it has affected the operating system (*ie* the social, political and cultural environments), but we have left to one side the ecclesiastical environment. But discussion of the local churches' management cannot be realistic unless this ecclesiastical environment is considered.

When we do this, the status of the local church is under examination. By our attention we have conveyed our conviction that it is important, but how does it compare with the other church systems? Our answer may be deduced from the way we have developed the oscillation theory. This could only be studied at the place where people actually engaged in religious activity, and the situation in Britain where this occurs for the majority is the local church. Because we cannot locate any other comparable point of interaction between religion and society we are forced to the conclusion that the local church is not only an institutional setting for religion, but *the* institutional setting as far as the christian churches go.

Arguments against the local church
This conclusion is strongly challenged by some who offer alternative structures. Three of these views demand consideration.

1. The local church is largely irrelevant
The argument is that life is so segmented, and people take

up so many different roles that to base the centre of religious activity on the place where people live is fallacious. Families are less important groupings for many people than their employment or their membership of special interest groups and provision by the church authorities for encounter in these groups satisfies a greater need than do home-based churches, particularly now that for most of the day all the family is away at work or at school. The substitute offered is the setting up of particular services in the context of the working life or to provide guidance and support for times of crisis. These include industrial advisors, counselling services, and midday church services. Our response is that there may be a good reason for some such initiatives but they cannot operate as satisfactory substitutes for local churches. They may be considered as particular types of evangelism.

Certainly if our conception of dependence is right, there is a need to regress to extra-dependence where opportunities are provided for primitive fantasy experiences in S-activity. The home may be half empty but at least it focusses dependence and can point to the church in the locality as a greater focus; whereas work mobilises fight in W-activity. As Industrial Chaplains learned in past years, they could not induce any real depth to religious life in such an environment, and though counselling and therapy offer dependent environments they can deal only with personal as distinct from corporate issues, and treat the client more as sick than as healthy. Thus while there are positive aspects to such ministries there are limitations which make them inadequate as settings for functional religious behaviour.

2. The local church is too small and self-centred

These critics believe that the survival needs of the local church causes people to segregate themselves away from the major concern in the community, and that church activities are really largely irrelevant. The local church therefore ties up too many human and material assets in catering for small groups who want to find a refuge from the social changes and convulsions going on around them. This critical attitude has resulted in efforts to redeploy these resources in other ways through, for example, policies of amalgamation.

The argument for centralisation comes from sociologists and management consultants whose view of organisational models is derived from other institutions where it is important to redeploy resources in order to achieve efficiency. But is it efficient to deprive a village of its own church services? It may be necessary because of financial constraints and be a sign of the church's failure, but there is no evidence that to combine churches into a group makes for efficacy except in an administrative sense, for example in providing adequate stipends for clergy. If a church has been the symbol of extra-dependence for a village, to deprive them of it is to cut out its heart. To put a contrary view we would say that if the church felt that maximum contact with people at the local level was the most valuable way for the church to carry out its mission or primary task, then it could set about cutting back in other ways to enable many smaller churches to continue to function.

Structure follows function in a mission. But those leading the tidying up process seem to have failed to interpret the complex role of communal churches of fifty years ago, and they have imposed theoretical models of the purpose of the church based wholly on the christian movement and neglecting process altogether. The re-organisation of small communal churches to form larger units in the expectation of better attended services with more professional clergy and increased opportunities for evangelism and social action, plays into the hands of pluralistic tendencies by weakening community responsibility and accountability, so that people feel alienated. The frequent result is the trend towards associational churches and further erosion of the church's capacity to represent the whole local community.

3. The local church is too large and formal

On the other hand, many churchgoers are complaining that they cannot breathe in large groups and withdraw from the established services of the local congregation to informal groupings or Christians in private homes or on church premises. The argument justifying this action is that the parish church is too big, too rigid and too stuffy and that for a vital personal experience of Christ a small group meeting is necessary. They maintain that since Christians are called to love one another, they need to know one another, and to know one another they must meet. They do so for discussion, prayer, scripture readings, spiritual healing and the Eucharist. Such informality overrides denominational boundaries and by-passes church regulations about intercommunion. Because these groups are often initiated and led by laity, many clergy will gladly support them, even if it means they do not attend church.

As long as such groups can remain spontaneous and evoke frank human interaction they are valuable, particularly if they include those who have insight into the personal needs of others. Sadly these groups frequently become more formal and exclusive than the congregations they criticized. Groups develop their own rituals and ways of talking. In other words they evolve their own form of religion, albeit a limited one because it cannot identify with the failings and weakness of other members of the Body of Christ since it has left them.

Small group meetings usually depend for their continuance on the enthusiasm of one or two members and when these people lose interest or move away the group may disintegrate, with the result that those that remain may become even more disillusioned and less capable of finding from the 'official' church the support they require.

In effect these small groups are associational churches and if they do not collapse they may eventually grow into one with its own form of ministry. If so what the members did to the church may happen to them – a secession. The major defect of this small group structure is that it is narcissistic and self-centred, and therefore its members do not contribute to apostolic religious behaviour even though they may be devout Christians. They represent no one but themselves so they either accept the societal values of their class environment unconsciously, or else reject them for their own. They have placed themselves in a position where they cannot work constructively with others about such values to modify or replace them.

There are two further arguments against the local church which need discussion. Neither offers alternative structures, so much as points in a different direction to what is in their opinion already there.

1. The basic church unit is the diocese or district

This argument is based on ecclesiastical definitions. Because the bishop is seen in episcopally governed churches as the key role in the presentation of the apostolic ministry, it follows, so the argument runs, that his jurisdiction, the diocese (or in some other denominations, the judicatory) is the basic unit of the church, and each parish church is only a segment of that whole. The point is also made that the voice of the bishop has considerable status in society, and by comparison the average local minister is without any real power.

The diocese/district and its leader have great importance for the 'faithful' of that denomination, but with few exceptions these church leaders have comparatively little importance for the community as a whole; neither has the diocese much meaning for the general population. By comparison the local church is an evident symbol for the surrounding community who interact with it either directly or indirectly. Cathedrals, in the general estimation of people, stand not for the diocese, but for the city they frequently dominate.

The diocese and the parish are geographical areas, or territories indicating the extent of the jurisdiction of bishop and clergy. It is our contention that the parish church is an operating unit carrying out the primary task of the churches, and the parish is the natural catchment area from which members come to participate in its activities.

2. The only church is the Body of Christ universal

Earlier we referred to the teaching of the invisible church. Its application here is to say that the local churches are only visible particles of a great whole, and that these parts are vessels like disposable cups. People advocating this view maintain that going to church as an act is irrelevant unless it brings the worshipper into the true church. The boundary between the local church and society is unimportant. The essential boundary to cross is between non-membership and membership of Christ's mystical Body. Hence the siting of a church, its rituals and ceremonies are of minor importance and, with deference to proprietary rights, can be constantly altered to suit current needs and attitudes. Those who resist are not likely to be representing any genuine christian reason, but only their own prejudices.

Anyone who has surveyed a number of churches in city areas is bound to feel the weight of this position. It is a greater act of faith to believe these sparsely-attended, decaying buildings are housing the basic unit of the church, than to believe in the invisible Church in all its power. Our response is that the half-alive inner-city church is not just a part, but according to the New Testament can be envisaged as the torn and broken Body of Christ and that its members are saints. Otherwise Paul is mistaken, for he speaks of heretical, lascivious and rebellious churches in these terms in his letters to the Corinthian and Colossian churches, to name two of them. If a church behaved like the Corinthians did in Paul's day, then any bishop would close it immediately!

Some would have no difficulty in accepting our conclusion that the local church is the proper institutional setting for religion, because they act as independent churches, though they have formal denominational links – the United Reformed Church and the churches of the Baptist Union for example. In the United States the churches of the major Protestant denominations would probably all come into this category. Other churches which are totally independent also support us. By our definition associational churches would support this view for reasons differing from those of communal type churches. The reasons for the former are fairly obvious: local autonomy, in matters of appointment and payment of clergy; local financing; and, within certain doctrinal limits, local programming. What we want to investigate primarily, however, are the implications for churches of the communal type. In so doing we believe we shall also have much to say about other types of churches.

Apostolic and diaconal systems

In order to investigate the objectives of the communal church it is necessary to engage in some organisational model-building (for the convention employed, see Rice (1963); Miller and Rice (1967); and Miller and Gwynne (1972), especially chapters 9 and 11).

Model A (Diagram 4A below) is similar to Diagram 2 (p. 148), and shows the worshipping group attending a particular service as the 'throughput' of the operating system. The human and material resources of the system (*eg* clergy, choir, furnishings, books) are deployed to facilitate the worshippers' regression to extra-dependence and transformation in intra-dependence. Since the attendance at church services varies from week to week, and many of the human resources are volunteers, each Sunday and each service requires, in principle, a separate model:

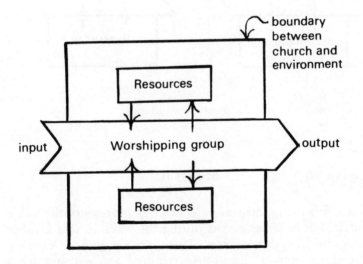

Diagram 4A   **Model A**

The next diagram represents a local church which has one act of worship each Sunday, over a two-week period:

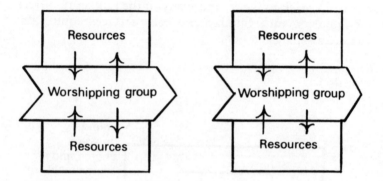

Diagram 4B **Model B**

The following diagram (Model C) represents the same church, but includes events during the week in which other groups use church resources. These include groups (X) using different resources than those required for worship (*eg* a house prayer group, a drama group), groups (Y) using some of the same resources as those used for Sunday worship (*eg* a mid-week Communion service, in church or in a home), and members of the congregation (Z) engaging in worship activities comparable to the Sunday services (*eg* a sick communion):

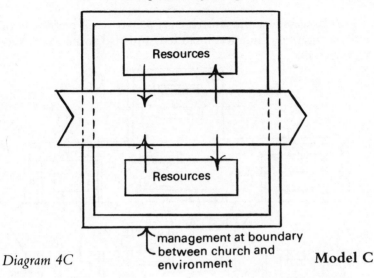

Diagram 4C   **Model C**

Model D, below, includes the management function in the basic model, model A. This is represented as a function at the boundary of the event, relating what happens in it to the environment from which the worshippers come:

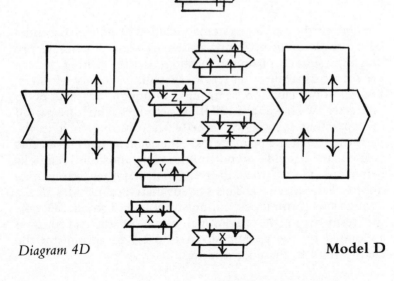

Diagram 4D   **Model D**

Finally we show the church over a two-week period, with the management function included, and also some of the service systems:

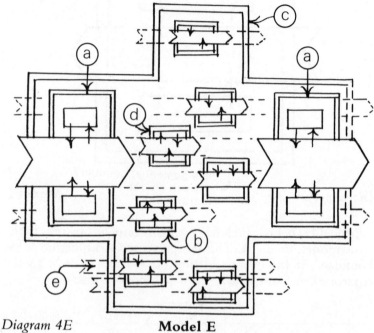

Diagram 4E   **Model E**

Some of the service systems included in Model E contribute directly to the operating system (*eg* choir practice, clergy meeting, service planning meeting, parish visiting by the priest/pastor) while other service systems do not (*eg* Mothers' Union, youth club, house groups), although they may do so indirectly. We have called all those activities which are part of the operating system, or directly contributing to it in the performance of the primary task, the *apostolic system*, since its task is to provide opportunities for apostolic religious behaviour. We regard all the remaining activities as constituting the *diaconal system*. This system therefore includes all the various sub-committees, administration, and so on. We take the term from the traditional name of the seven men appointed by the apostles in Acts 6:2-4 to administer the charity fund to the poor widows.

The enterprise management in the Church of England would be the Parochial Church Council, and it would be involved in both apostolic and diaconal systems. One of the difficulties any church councillor, deacon or steward knows is the ease with which the diaconal system pushes out the work of the apostolic system. The parish priest would have leadership roles in the apostolic system by virtue of his leadership of the operating system of worship (a), clergy meetings (b), sick visiting (d), etc. and his chairmanship of the PCC (c) which he might share with a Lay Chairman. He would have a leadership role in the diaconal system by virtue of the PCC (c), and a membership role in that system if, say, he attended a house group (e).

The large number of roles he has to take makes it difficult to change attitudes from one to the other, particularly if the laity want to 'fix' him in the 'priest' role, so that even if he attends as a member, a group will be unable to see him except as 'our priest'. This may tempt him to go to excessive lengths to show he is one of the boys, and so shatter the laity's image of him that they now find it difficult to see him in the priest role even during the services. His position is further complicated because in the operating system the prevailing mode is extra-dependence, and S-activity is dominant, but in the diaconal system the appropriate mode is intra-dependence, with W-activity dominant. Even if he is skilled enough to mobilise the changed attitude in himself he may find that some members of the PCC cannot focus on work in W-activity, and drift towards extra-dependence where S-activity is dominant, and therefore important decisions are not taken.

The church's management group is generally elected by the full members of the local church, and at least annually is responsible to them for its performance. In some denominations where there are associational churches they exercise a very firm hold on its officers, and could be regarded as a superordinate management body which, if it were in industry, would be the shareholders. (The analogy is not by any means exact because the shareholders of a chocolate factory are neither the girls packing them, nor the chocolates being packed!) In a communal church the management group is generally much freer and probably feels more accountable to the vicar than to the congregation.

The local church and its ecclesiastical environment

The management council, board or meeting not only has to manage the internal life of the local church but also the relations between the church and the outside world. This means vetting the types of people who use the church resources; are there any groups to which it would not let the hall for example?

The superordinate structure of the local church is so different between the denominations that again we will use the Church of England as a case study. In the early third century the terms for parish and diocese were interchangeable as the domain of a bishop. The bishop with the parish priest is nowadays jointly responsible for the well-being of the parish, as the bishop in his Solemn Commission to the new incumbent in the Institution Service entrusts him with 'the care of souls which is both thine and mine'. The bishop is part of the apostolic system but how does he relate to hundreds of parishes to carry out that responsibility? Obviously the bishop cannot be there in his own person very frequently no matter how hard he works. If his physical presence were essential we should have many more bishops with smaller dioceses. The present plan of having several area bishops is an unsatisfactory half measure. In some deaneries the rural dean is encouraged to become a mini-bishop but a recent study (Hutton and Reed, 1975) showed that this was generally unacceptable to the clergy as a substitute for the bishop himself.

Two other possibilities remain. One is to regard the bishop's role as equivalent to that of a managing director, the other is based on the concept of corporate representation. There are three assumptions behind the managing director model of the role. The first is that a centralised policy has authority over departmental heads, the role corresponding to the parish incumbent. But the priest, although bound to obey the bishop canonically, considers the parish to be his responsibility and his performance cannot be added up statistically with that of other parish priests and audited against a business plan. In no way does the priest behave like a departmental head. The second assumption is that there is a chain of command through which the managing director manages and controls. But synodical government at diocesan and deanery level, because it does not directly work with the primary task, is directed not to the parish priest in the apostolic system, but to him and the PCC in the diaconal system. Thirdly, the managing director role is based on the principle that the departmental manager will act as his substitute, so that the managing director need *not* be there. There would be hollow laughs on the shop floor if their manager invoked the managing director to support his own instructions, because in their eyes it would be a sign of his weakness. The inadequacy of this model for the church is discussed below.

The other possible structure is based on corporate representation, by which we mean that where the part is, there is the whole, one and undivided. We have seen that this is a principle present in different ways in human relations, and in assumptions about the church. In the realm of psychology we arrived at the hypothesis that one person could represent another in consciously engaging in the oscillation process, especially in participating in the extra-dependent mode. In the sphere of the symbolic language of theology the Body of Christ is fully represented in each member; if one suffers, all suffer, if one is honoured all rejoice together (I Cor 12:26). The bishop and his clergy share in the cure of souls at the parish level, and we suggest that the bishop is present with each parish priest in the conducting of the worship in the apostolic system. Three pieces of evidence support this contention. The bishop is present in that he has declared in the church, either directly or through the archdeacon, that the cure of souls is shared with the new incumbent, so he accepts responsibility for being there in the parish. Secondly he, or his brother bishops, have laid hands on the priest, and thus the bishop's authority is celebrated when the priest leads the Eucharist. Thirdly, all those members of the Church of England who receive communion do so through episcopal laying on of hands, and so communicant members celebrate the bishop's presence with them. Parish churches also have bishop's chairs or cathedra so each of them can be at least in fantasy his cathedral.

This is our interpretation of what is already happening. It does not have to be made to happen, but to be understood by the parties involved. The notion is of one piece with the theory of the primary task of the church, and if that is grasped by the bishop and the parish priest then this conception will be illuminated for them. Bishops experience great pressure from the laity to be present in person and they will need some convincing, but we have already posed more difficult tasks for the priest in describing his role. Parish priests might well contemplate the thought that, if the laity want to meet the bishop, perhaps they have not enabled them to come sufficiently close to God in the extra-dependent mode in the liturgy. The managing director appoints the manager so that he, the managing director, *will not need* to be there in the department; the bishop institutes a parish priest in order that he *will* be there in the parish.

The significance of this is that the bishop serves the parish, not that the parish serves the diocese, and we can conceive of a diocese in the apostolic system as a domain wholly covered by parishes in each of which the bishop presides with the parish priest. If the churches lack assurance of their authority here is a way to regain it. The ancient bishop/presbyter role is re-affirmed, with the bishop sub-role being to preserve the apostolic tradition so that the churches are firmly rooted in the historic symbolism of the christian movement; and the presbyter sub-role being to conduct the acting-out of that symbolism in ritual so that Christians are firmly rooted in their communities as fully human.

In the apostolic system we can therefore speak of the bishop's role as 'bishop-in-parish', which matches his role as Chairman of the Diocesan synod, as 'bishop-in-synod', in which role he leads the diocesan diaconal system. This system comprises deanery synods, diocesan boards and committees, patronage, and the work of such officials as suffragan bishops, chancellors, archdeacons, registrars, and rural deans, as well as advisers and directors of specialist functions like industry and education. If the bishop can see the value in disentangling these two roles we predict he will be able to identify his priorities more readily, and if he does not accede, at least as easily, to the increasing demands of the diaconal system, he will be strengthening his clergy to do likewise by his example.

The difficulty that lay representatives have in changing from the diaconal system role to the apostolic system role and vice versa, is an interesting comment on the oscillation process which implies that there are central points in the transition from one mode to the other represented by these two task systems. Hence, if laity find it hard to change roles from a W-activity dominated system to an S-activity dominated system, it justifies the need for tough training for clergy to enable them to do it, so that they can make it possible for others.

A fuller treatment of these superordinate structures of dioceses, presbyteries, districts and judicatories needs to be carried out. Our intention has been to open up a line of discussion which could allow for the integration of functional religious behaviour into the structure of the various denominations.

A Personal Postscript: Churches in Crisis

What we set out to do remains unfinished. We hope however that there may be those who will share with us the task of carrying the arguments further, applying them in new situations in which their validity can be tested.

The contents and shape of this book have a long history. They emerge from three interlinked experiences. The first occurred in 1952 when in Finland I first read Moreno's *Who Shall Survive?* (1934). Reading this I was aware that the interactions between human beings in a group were not sufficiently explained by numbering their interactions and assigning some qualitative score to them.

The second experience occurred five years later when I took part in what was known as a 'group life laboratory'. The programme included one event in which members met together to examine their reactions to each other within a group. In trying to understand the way I was interacting with other people I had the feeling that I was sharing with them a feeling of 'something' outside myself. I was unsure whether the something was outside the group or within it. But the feeling was strong enough to make us aware that our behaviour as individuals was being influenced by it.

There was no apparent reason for this behaviour, but I became aware that it posed a significant question. As a practising Christian I believed in God and knew what it felt like to worship in church. What puzzled me was that the feelings generated in worship which I had attributed to faith in God were very similar to those I experienced in the group sessions. I was confronted with the question as to whether I was being deluded in my faith or in some way was God actually manifesting himself in the group?

I tried to read what I could about the behaviour of small groups. It was suggested by some authors that groups passed through different phases in their development. The first phase was stated as being one of 'dependence' and intellectually I could accept that there was some correlation between the group in finding something to depend on, and the Christian church in having faith in God.

Up to this stage I was keeping my faith in God separate from my experience in the group, using the latter to illustrate rather than to investigate the nature of my reliance upon God. The way ahead seemed to be blocked until in 1962 I engaged in another group activity. Here I became aware that the group members were engaged in the joint activity of creating their own religion as a way of surviving in the face of their anxieties as a group about its disintegration. I was compelled to examine what I meant by faith in, or dependence upon, God. Was this faith merely the result of my own human need, or did it relate to some external intervention by God from outside human experience?

The questions raised by these experiences led me to investigate human behaviour in actual situations and to study sociology, psychology and anthropology, placing the findings of these disciplines alongside my previous theological knowledge. This reaching out into diverse fields was a search for meaning, meaning about the place of dependence in human existence.

The contents of this book represent some of the thoughts which have evolved through that investigation. I am aware that the 'new' ideas and dreams of those years seem less convincing and colourful now that they have been presented for others to peruse and examine. As Ehrenzweig (1967) has pointed out, all authorship results in mourning, because something is lost in what he calls the 'secondary revisions' as thoughts are marshalled for publication. Who knows what attacks these brain-children will receive, or to what oblivion they may be sent, unread.

My response to these experiences was not only a matter of reflection. My professional work in advising others in leadership and organisation kept me alert to the turbulence of the world in which we live. The act of creativity was not principally a matter of bringing order out of chaos, in order to reduce the complexity by capturing it on paper. Creativity was something different. It was the opening up of the possibilities of this line of thinking, offering the new dimensions of experience in order that action might take place.

The book has deposited us, author and reader alike, in this place of uncertainty. Though it has not yet ended, we have imposed an ending. Yet prospects have opened up which make us impatient to go further. It means walking unsteadily along the brink of confusion and discovery, knowing that if we could stop being afraid of the uncertainty we would find satisfaction in this mystery. For me these ideas are starting-points for new investigations, for testing, for confirming and perhaps for developing.

The following pages represent a personal attempt to come to grips with some of the questions which are facing the christian churches in Britain. As we have said in the opening chapter, this focusing down on the UK is not intended to eliminate or to separate out other nations and religions. It is rather a way of giving specific interpretations about current issues, in order that those who are interested may be able to make their own adaptations.

The churches in crisis

When symbols lose their potency they can no longer shape experience. The simple cross symbol can be so potent that a mere glimpse of it evokes thoughts of crucifixion and the resurrection of Jesus. In Western nations it is becoming only a decoration, an empty symbol, which like the person cleansed of one demon is now ready to be invaded by seven others, and become a magical sign or a talisman.

The fate of the cross has embraced him who hung upon it. The mention of his name can terrify evil-doers and heal the sick, but for many he has been stripped of his messianic glory and emptied of his sense of mission, so that like a golliwog he is filled up with notions which someone wants to justify; he becomes a guerilla fighter, say, or a homosexual. A stage has been reached where people reading the Gospels for the first time react negatively against the Jesus portrayed there, and reject the image of God he offers. While popular use of the words 'Jesus', 'Christ', 'cross', no longer necessarily inclines the hearer or observer towards the christian movement, the New Testament still has the power to arouse strong emotions even if the current behaviour is to turn against Jesus and crucify him afresh.

Primitive pagan symbols once baptised into the christian movement like Easter, the goddess, are stirring the unconscious afresh, so these symbols are coming forth from the depths and hollows with new energy. The archaic symbolic meanings which derived from the process itself are therefore breaking through the christian re-interpretation of them. The violent changes in our social and political behaviour have like an earthquake opened up deep chasms across the face of a culture apparently contented with its christian values, and forces and powers are being released from our own selves which makes us fear for the future. Feverishly we are groping after ways of surviving and are only too ready to grasp at any symbol which can offer hope, which is probably why TV advertising is so successful.

Religious behaviour is difficult to interpret. The following description of an Anglican service is disturbing in this connection:

During the Eucharist the congregation became more and more intense. The service was pregnant with feeling and concern which caused me to become deeply involved. As the time for receiving communion approached I tried to focus on the Christ who takes our broken lives and who in giving his broken body, restores us to wholeness again, but instead I found myself filled up with consciousness of the people around me and their relations with each other. The manifest dignity of the service held me tight in this human inter-communion to the suppression of my traditional christian ideas. Afterwards I learnt that I had not wholly imagined it, because this was the intention of many of those present.

The ambiguity of meaning in such services leaves us unsure as to whether it was celebrating liberation through human fellowship in general, or if it was a coming together around christian symbols to give thanks for the self-giving of Jesus and to enter into union with him.

Christian churches are confronted with a great problem. Are they in a position to serve the oscillation process of a society by promoting functional religious behaviour? How strong is the evidence to show that some churches are now being used as centres of folk religion which is openly taking over the sacred symbols from the christian movement, and that other churches are withdrawing into themselves, being concerned principally for themselves, and thereby having to suppress those aspects of the Gospel which call them to be concerned for all men? Where are the churches who do accept their accountability to humanity in the name of God who became man?

These questions are raised by our theory of religion as we see it applied to the current social situation in which we live in Britain. Before we respond to them, there are one or two preliminary observations. We have remarked on the great increase over the last fifty years of groups and activities centred on churches which are largely restricted to members and their contacts, and have interpreted them as a sign of the failure on the part of the church members to experience the profound satisfaction of contemplating God, thereby providing a transition to full engagement in day to day life. Many Christians have felt hurt and misunderstood by this conclusion, protesting that they are not avoiding the world but preparing better to face it. Why have they reacted like this? One possible reason is the realisation that there is a difference between the intention and the fact; witness, for example, the acute disappointment of some clergy and key church workers when a prospective leader of activities says that he cannot afford the time to attend their particular group, because of his commitment to other forms of service in the community. Another reason is seen by examining the type of person who engages in the church centred activities; they usually are not the most influential members of the town. If they do attend church, usually they are quietly modest about it, which may indicate that those running the activities are trying to compensate for something lacking in themselves. Probably however the strongest reason for their protest is that their security is threatened. The activities have been made into a fence to protect themselves against the world and its influence, and to justify their wish to look inwards. If such people were to accept that their behaviour shows that they are lame and need crutches, they would rejoice when they knew that there was a way to walk so that their props could be thrown aside, but instead their self-image is one of spiritual strength, of a mature faith, not, as Paul would have called it, 'weak faith' (Rom. 14:1f).

Paul goes on to say, 'It is not for outsiders like us to rush in and pull the fences down, but it is our responsibility to point out the effects of that behaviour.' Two effects are very important. This hyperactive behaviour prevents the members of society from using churches to deal with their dependent problems where they or their representatives can regress to dependence. The fastest growing churches in both Britain and the United States are the fundamentalists who specifically repulse any compromise between themselves and their environments. Within their own churches they can only tolerate those who accept their own clear-cut norms and principles. To them the concept of vicarious oscillation is thought to be dangerous and even as heretical. These churches are models of associational churches and as such are growing at the expense of the communal type. Individually many church members would consider themselves concerned about the world and its needs and exemplify this by the work they undertake, but basically their only answer to it is that other men and women should be as they are and that salvation for eternity involves a form of separation in this life. Our concern is that in saving their own souls they are in effect shutting others out. Those shut out have to look elsewhere for religious satisfaction and do so by demystifying the dependence symbolism from christian mythology and imagery. Progressively therefore the churches have less and less attraction as a way of focussing the nation's dependence. Such churches are direct descendants of those men to whom Jesus is reported to have said:

You shut the Kingdom of Heaven against men; for you

neither enter yourselves, nor allow those who would enter to go in. (Matt 23:13)

The other effect is that such hyper-active behaviour is extremely wasteful. It is undeniably attractive to engage in such soul-satisfying activities, and therefore people are ready to invest time and money in setting up and maintaining complex establishments. If our hypothesis fits the facts, then these resources are actually a handicap for the churches, and the members and their leaders would do well to consider terminating most of them, retaining only those which directly service the apostolic system of the local church. Because a great many properties could be sold off, the financial burden of the churches would be greatly eased and energy could be concentrated on servicing church worship and pastoral action.

Another observation is about evangelism, and what the oscillation theory implies about it. We are engaged in the study of human behaviour and our approach is to begin with the natural process of oscillation and lead in to the examination of the movement. The evangelist's approach is to begin with movement and apply it to process, but sometimes process is disregarded. In the New Testament era the churches had to exhibit the potency of the christian symbols and to demonstrate how their acting out in ritual penetrated to the heart of human need. But we cannot with integrity merely read off the behaviour of the early churches and try to reproduce it today, because the environmental conditions are different. In the apostolic era the processes in the various cultures of the Roman empire were alien to christian mythology. Now, at least in Europe and America, the process uses christian symbolism to shape its experience, even if the symbols are being given new meanings. But this usage, we believe, is rapidly changing, and will accelerate if the church leaders cannot display sufficient understanding of people who are bewildered and confused about religion. Under these conditions evangelism can easily degenerate into recruitment for churches which prevents other members from perceiving the comprehensive vision of life which the gospel can open up. This so-called evangelism is but a less extreme form of mind-bending, used by cults and sects on followers who are expected to abandon all organic links with their past and submit themselves to the strait-jacket of a movement which creates an artificial and unnatural process to fit in with its doctrines.

Opportunities for life
If we take up the questions we posed in earlier chapters, there are four points to consider if local churches are to take up the implications of the oscillation theory.

1. The churches as servants of society
Churches carrying out the primary task claim their work is for the benefit of the whole of society in that they are endeavouring to manage the dependent aspect of corporate life in order to free the community as a whole to cope with other aspects of human existence. The Gospel is entrusted to the churches on behalf of the world or to use John Calvin's term, they are God's stewards to show his care for the whole community through the church. This role is well recognised and enriched and expounded in the servant songs in Isaiah (Isaiah ch. 42-53) and in Paul's letters. Our emphasis includes the prophetic element which assesses the work of the churches not by their own behaviour, or the behaviour of their members in the wider context of society, but by questioning the dominant values which are recognised by the nation, embodied in its legislation and enjoyed by its citizens. In the world of politics and economics the church is small-time and amateur; but in leading worship and coping with the crisis transitions in life the churches possess the highest level of competence and skill. It is by their serving society in that capacity that the nation and its citizens will derive the greatest benefit.

2. Christians as human beings
Any enterprise worthy of the name wants to be pleased with its results. But it needs to use the same criterion as those who use its products. The second-hand car may look beautiful, but will it soon fall to pieces on the road? Churches have been

branding their products 'christian' since the beginning, a slang description originating from outsiders. But the real *package* is a regenerated human being, made in Jesus' likeness, to become one with mankind as he was. The mark of Jesus was his *oneness* with man, not his differences. His crucifixion was brought about not because he claimed to be unique and exercised special powers, but because he stubbornly went about his business, doing good where he could, and thereby revealing a totally new image of God. To employ the meanings we have attributed to authority and power (p. 168) the churches have generally been more interested in the *power* of its 'experts' in influencing others, than in the *authority* these 'experts' have as members of the Kingdom of God – authority to take a kingly role in the city of man, as Augustine would say, without being oblivious to the way that city is interpenetrated by the City of God (Augustine, *The City of God*, XIX. 13). Operating in this role, members can use the power they receive from God through the church to deploy it in furthering, not the church, but the State.

3. *The resources available to churches*
We consider the churches have amassed resources for objectives which have nothing to do with their task, and made unfounded assumptions about the priority of their operations which have caused them to neglect resources which are readily available to them. We are daunted by the complexity of this subject but want to offer the following observations. In countries where the symbols of the process have no christian content (*eg* Iran), any christian presence is sectarian, and the Islamic movement energises the process and deals with dependency. Churches in these countries are founded or continue only where there are sufficient Christians who wish to maintain them. The associational church is bound to be the initial model (see p. 157). However in countries where the christian movement deals with the social dependency, churches are essential to ensure the continuance of this task wherever there are people, for the sake of the nation. This issue is initially significant whenever there is a question either of closing existing churches, or of building new ones.

The fact that in England it is the closure of communal type

churches (*ie* Church of England churches), and not of associational churches (*ie* Free Churches), which raises problems for the community, provides some evidence for our case. It is an awkward and distressing problem today, because although the church authorities recognise the value of keeping some churches open, they consider they have not the resources to do so. Our contention is that they are viewing the issue from the wrong angle. Though the policy of the Church of England is officially to promote communal churches, the fantasy behind that policy held by its officials is frequently that of associational churches. The decision to close badly attended churches in order to attempt to create a larger and more active congregation seems to take its model from centralisation plans whose principles are derived from theoretical disciplines like operational research, instead of from an understanding of human need.

We offer four concrete proposals wherever there is a problem about providing church facilities for a community. First, that discussions take place to determine whether an existing church institution is serving the community task. If it is not, then close it; if it is, then church authorities should discuss with *all* the people in the area what can be done to keep it open.

Secondly, the number and general location of churches under threat should be kept before all the churches and the call should go out for clergy to take up posts in them. The next step would require the undoing of certain policies to do with stipends and housing. These borderline churches would be taken out of the standard policy and given permission to make other arrangements, so that clergy who wanted to respond to the call of such hard-pressed communities could be free to make their sacrifices of money, convenience and living accommodation. It has surprised us that no suggestion has been made, at least openly, about the desirability of encouraging the celibacy of clergy, because we are now at a time when many churches cannot afford married clergy with families.

Thirdly, a special fund should be opened to be made available for churches such as we have been discussing. This fund would mainly rely on capital raised when churches who became convinced of their community task could see the positive aspect of selling off their now redundant property. We are not advocating sudden death, but the withering away of these surplus activities and institutions. Undoubtedly some properties would be better transferred directly to the community, for example when the church hall is the only building large enough for community gatherings.

Fourthly, the opening up of new churches requires an existing community, or at least the beginnings of one. In a new estate where a community is gradually being accumulated some sign could be given to indicate that the church authorities are willing to co-operate with any local initiative. One way is for these authorities to take an option on land and erect a christian symbol such as a large cross on it, with a notice announcing that this site is available for development as a church when the people are ready, an action which could quicken the communal response, because they have a symbol which immediately begins to facilitate and support the regression to extra-dependence.

In areas where the proposal is to open up a new church we would suggest that this is not done without consultation with both the householders in the area and if possible with all other churches of the same, or different, denominations which are nearby. It is encouraging to know that this is no new suggestion, but perhaps the outcome of previous experiments has sometimes been disappointing because the communal aspect has not been prominent enough to dispel associational rivalry. Only a ruthless pursuit of the primary task of the church will cut through the tangles of misunderstanding between a church and its social setting, and between denominations. We are not prescribing a sure way to success, but an expression of integrity.

4. *New partners for old*

The growth of pluralism and other social changes have caused a shift in the way church denominations line up in relation to each other. Previously the major obstacle to co-operation between churches was the churches' own view of themselves, and the differences were those of church doctrine and polity – that is, concerning details of the christian movement. What is now becoming more significant is how churches are relating to society, and the differences between churches are those of social dynamics – that is, concerning details of the process. In some cities, towns and regions an intermediate position prevails where churches from different denominations, facing the same social problems, such as unemployment of young people, or lack of housing for the elderly, combine to sponsor social action.

The division between churches of the communal type and those of the associational type is the critical one. Church unions or partnerships among churches of the same type are those which are likely to be achieved, so in Britain two associational churches, the English Presbyterian and the Congregational Union, could manage to come together as the United Reformed Church. But the marriage between one dominantly communal type, the Church of England, and one associational type, the Methodist Church, failed. It is of significance that a grave impediment obstructing closer relations between the communal Roman Catholics and the communal Church of England has recently come through the associational Episcopal Church in America, which is in communion with the Church of England, approving the ordination of women.

However there are signs that as church denominations revise their liturgies they are drawing on common sources of inspiration, which makes it possible that with a deeper shared experience of worship some associational types at local level begin to drift towards the communal type. Likewise the charismatic movement, traditionally linked to associational types, has become manifest in the communal churches. We have encouraged churches in these pregnant situations to arrange for representatives to meet and compose a prayer for joint use about the welfare and development of their shared neighbourhood. The prayer expresses their collective accountability to the structures of the State to sustain it while simultaneously judging the conduct of its citizens as represented in the members of their congregations. Each church would incorporate the prayer in its weekly service, and then wait and see what happens in the community.

Warnings about destruction

'He that loses his soul for my sake and the Gospel's will save it' are Jesus' words to the churches, but that is not all he said. 'He that seeks to save his soul shall lose it' (Mark 8:35) is a prediction which the churches do well to ponder. If the christian movement is shunted into a siding, no other religious movement is likely to dominate Western society and provide a coherent pattern of symbols by which its values and culture can be shaped for the benefit of the whole. Otherwise our national life will degenerate into a cacophony of hymns and devotions to many deities while cults and mystery religions flourish in glades, caves and sitting-rooms.

But modern states cannot continue as wholes unless their cultures can be co-ordinated. If religion and the churches fail, they will be compelled to produce leaders from politics and the armed forces who will step in and establish civil religion. These psychological dynamics operated in the slave plantations of America and the concentration camps of Europe, when the disintegrated and disheartened slaves and prisoners were drawn irresistibly to have regard for those who had the power of life and death over them; they treated their guards like gods. This is no insubstantial dream for those who remember Stalin and Mao Tse Tung, but a prospective nightmare for those who believe in the validity of the christian movement. Because not everyone is a 'believer in the civil religion' in so-called totalitarian countries, westerners who consider themselves to be free like to generalise on the tales carried by 'unbelieving' refugees and regard their whole country as subject to evil bondage. But without disputing the personal experience of these refugees, the great mass of their fellow countrymen are probably more content than we would want to think.

The strength of the christian movement depends upon its capacity to generate a vocabulary of symbols which could be co-ordinated to cover all the contingencies of human existence. Its power would be demonstrated if there was no deep concern of the human psyche which could not respond to the Gospel, and no lofty aspiration of the spirit which it could not irradiate like the sun glancing on the wings of a kingfisher. But in practice some hitherto significant symbols are being discarded, especially those to do with the existence of evil, and those about life after death. Where this occurs, with revolution, torture and murder daily in the news, we can only conclude that it must mean that apart from a few lone voices, the mass of the churches are gradually becoming private clubs. Unless churches can experience potency in the resurrection symbol, and apply it themselves, they will wither away to triviality.

4.45 p.m., Sunday 6 June 1977
College of Preachers,
Washington, DC

Appendix

Patterns of relatedness in Bion's theory of small group behaviour

Bion (1961) suggests that in any small group it is possible to discern two types of mental activity. The first he called 'work-group' activity, and corresponds to our 'W-activity'. This is rational thought directed towards carrying out the task for which the group has been constituted. This is either obstructed or assisted by another kind of mental activity which becomes intelligible if it is taken to spring from 'basic assumptions', which are usually unconscious, held in common by all members of the group. This may be seen as directed towards defending the individual against anxieties about the survival of the group. It is referred to by Bion as 'basic assumption' activity, and corresponds to our 'S-activity'.

Bion describes three recurring *basic assumptions* each of which gives rise to characteristic patterns of relatedness, between group members and between leader and members. These are:

i) that the group's survival depends upon being sustained and protected by an all-powerful, all-knowing leader (who may be a person, present or absent, an institution, or an idea). Bion calls this basic assumption *dependence*.

ii) that the group's survival depends upon producing a new leader (who may be a person, institution or idea) who will deliver them from their present difficulties. Groups frequently produce pairs of members who are regarded as though they are the potential parents of this new Messiah. Bion therefore called this basic assumption *pairing*, though the term *expectancy* might be preferable.

iii) that the group's survival depends upon destroying or evading an enemy (person, institution or idea) which threatens it. This is basic assumption *fight-flight*.

Dependence

When the group's pattern of relatedness is based on the dependence assumption, members behave as though they had access to a person or object which is able to supply all their needs, without their having to do anything except wait and receive. Correspondingly, they feel themselves to be weak, ignorant, inadequate and vulnerable. Capacities which they are able to use elsewhere disappear in the climate of dependence.

When the group has projected its shared idea of an all-powerful leader onto someone present in the group, what he actually says and does is bound sooner or later to be a disappointment, since he is a fallible human being. The group therefore has to work hard, against the evidence, to maintain the fantasy on which, it is felt, their survival depends. When the leader's behaviour does not fit the role he has been cast in, it is ignored or explained away. Another member may be unconsciously assigned the role of a disciple or high priest who explains and justifies the words and actions of the leader to the other members. Alternatively the leader may be manipulated to show the love and power he appears to be hiding, by giving him problems to solve, or patients on whom to demonstrate his skill.

In some groups the fantasy of the super-human leader can be maintained indefinitely, with the collusion of the one cast in the role. If he insists on his fallibility, or when evidence for this becomes too great to be ignored, the group disposes of him abruptly. It is then faced with finding another magic leader, or with securing its survival in some other way.

Expectancy (Pairing)

Sometimes the group turns its attention to fostering the hope that a new leader or new era is about to appear, which will deliver the group from its present difficulties. Action is directed towards maintaining this atmosphere of expectancy, and thus suppressing feelings of depression, destructiveness or despair which might otherwise emerge. No realistic action is taken to bring about the imagined new state of affairs, since the group already enjoys it in fantasy. The qualities of the leader are similar to those of the leader of the dependent group, but his lineaments are rather those of a hero, a Messiah, a Che Guevara. He is an object of hope rather than veneration. An organisation which is short of staff frequently invests a coming new member of staff with Messianic hopes of this kind. His qualities are magnified, his inevitable limitations ignored, and it is supposed that when he arrives the present state of over-work and lack of support will be a thing of the past.

Bion observed that in this mood groups frequently become engrossed in the relationship between two members, as though they were to be the parents of the new leader, or would produce the magic solution between them. Perhaps a more important variant of this is the group which builds up an atmosphere of hope and idealism by fostering intimate inter-personal relationships. The group is a pattern of shifting pairs, between members of the same and of opposite sexes. This leads to a shared idea of a group which is highly idealised. All the negative aspects of human relationships are projected outside the group, onto external authorities, careers, marriages and social systems.

Fight-Flight

The key element in the fight-flight pattern is that there is no dependable leader or institution in view. The group falls back upon impulsive attack and defence to secure the survival of its members. The group switches abruptly from fight to flight in response to supposed threats and opportunities to attack. It selects as its leader a member with paranoid tendencies, who is constitutionally prone to identify enemies, and he leads the search-and-destroy operation. People, ideas and institutions so identified are mercilessly divested of power and demolished. Alternatively, if the group invests them with power as well as hostility, it engages in activities which take the group, in fantasy, out of the danger area. For example, a class or committee which is presented with a new idea which calls into question their cherished beliefs, may either pour scorn on the idea without endeavouring to understand it, or divert the discussion into another, safer area.

A group dominated by this basic assumption communicates in crude slogans and is impatient of any pause for thought. Its ideal is the charge of the Light Brigade: 'Theirs not to reason why, Theirs but to do and die ... ' Whereas the dependent group is afraid of hurting or losing members, since this calls into question the over-arching care of its leader, the fight-flight group regards its members as cannon-fodder, and is reckless of casualties. The emergence of this basic assumption in on-going groups and institutions is often indicated by increased lateness, absenteeism, and threats of resignation.

References

Augustine (c 426). *The City of God*

Augustine (399). *Confessions*, London: Dent (Everyman Edition) (1907)

Balint, M. (1968). *The Basic Fault – Therapeutic Aspects of Regression*, London: Tavistock

Barbour, I. G. (1974). *Myths, Models and Paradigms*, London: SCM Press

Barth, K. (1928). *The Word of God and the Word of Man*, London: Hodder & Stoughton

Bateson, G. (1973). *Steps to an Ecology of Mind*, St Albans, Hertfordshire: Paladin

Bede (c 700). *A History of the English Church and People*, Harmondsworth: Penguin (1955)

Berger P. and Luckmann T. (1963). 'Sociology of religion and sociology of knowledge', *Sociology and Social Research*, vol. 47.
    Reproduced in Robertson R (ed.) (1969). *Sociology of Religion*, Harmondsworth: Penguin

Berger P. (1967). *The Sacred Canopy*, New York: Doubleday. Published in England as *The Social Reality of Religion*, London: Faber (1969)

Bertalanffy L. von (1968). *General System Theory*, Harmondsworth: Penguin (1973)

Bettelheim B. (1967). *The Empty Fortress*, New York: Free Press

Bettis J. D. (ed.) (1969). *Phenomenology of Religion*, London: SCM Press

Bion, W. R. (1961). *Experiences in Groups*, London: Tavistock

Bion, W. R. (1965). *Transformations*, London: Heinemann

Bion, W. R. (1970). *Attention and Interpretation*, London: Tavistock

Bonhoeffer, D. (1949). *Life Together*, Munich: Chr. Kaiser Verlag; London: SCM Press (1954)

Bowlby J. (1969). *Attachment and Loss, Vol 1 Attachment*, London: Hogarth Press and Institute of Psycho-Analysis

Bowlby, J. (1973). *Attachment and Loss, Vol 2 Loss*, London: Hogarth Press and Institute of Psycho-Analysis

Confucius. *Analects*

Cox, H. (1965). *The Secular City*, London: SCM Press

Cupitt, D. (1976). Broadcast reported in *The Listener,* August 1976, London: British Broadcasting Corporation

Dahrendorf, R. (1974). Sixth 1974 Reith Lecture, 'Steps in the right direction', *The Listener*, 2 January 1975, London: British Broadcasting Corporation

Douglas, M. (1970). *Natural Symbols – Explorations in Cosmology*, London: Barrie and Rockliff, the Cresset Press

Douglas, M. (1966). *Purity and Danger: An Analysis of Concepts of Pollution and Taboo*, London: Routledge and Kegan Paul; Harmondsworth: Penguin (1970)

Durkheim, E. (1893). *The Division of Labour in Society*. English translation: New York: The Free Press (1947)

Durston, D. M. K. (1972). Project on the Task of the Local Church, (1968-1972). Field notes in the possession of the Grubb Institute

Ehrenzweig, A. (1967). *The Hidden Order of Art*, St Albans, Hertfordshire: Paladin (1970)

Eliade, M. (1957). *The Sacred and the Profane*, New York: Harcourt, Brace & World (1959)

Emanuel, J. (1977). 'Italy's private cults', London: *The Tablet*, 9 April 1977, p. 356

Emery, F. E. (1970). *Freedom and Justice within Walls*, London: Tavistock

Emery, F. E. and Trist, E. L. (1973). *Towards a Social Ecology*, New York: Plenum Press, paperback edition (1975)

Erikson, E. (1968). *Identity – Youth and Crisis*, New York: W. W. Norton; London: Faber

Freud, S. (1911). *Formulations on the Two Principles of Mental Functioning*, Standard Edition, Vol 12, London: Hogarth Press and Institute of Psycho-Analysis (1958)

Freud, S. (1927). *The Future of an Illusion*, Standard Edition, Vol. 21, London: Hogarth Press and Institute of Psycho-Analysis

Hartmann, H. (1958). *Ego Psychology and the Problem of Adaptation*, New York: International University Press; London: Imago

Holt, J. (1967). *How Children Learn*, USA: Pitman; Harmondsworth: Penguin (1970)

Hutton, J. M. and Reed, B. D. (1975). *The Rural Deanery*, London: The Grubb Institute (duplicated)

Jung, C. G. (1940). *The Integration of the Personality*, London: Kegan Paul

Jung, C. G. (1959). *The Archetypes and the Collective Unconscious*, (Collected Works, Volume 9)

Kahn, M. M. R. (1974). *The Privacy of the Self*, London: Hogarth Press and Institute of Psycho-Analysis

Kierkegaard, S. (1844). *The Concept of Dread*, Princeton: Princeton University Press (1957)

Kris, E. (1952). *Psychoanalytic Explorations in Art*, New York: International University Press; New York: Schocken Books (1964)

Laing, R. D. (1961). *The Self and Others*, London: Tavistock

Lake, F. (1966). *Clinical Theology*, London: Darton, Longman and Todd

Langer, Susanne K. (1942). *Philosophy in a New Key*, Cambridge, Mass.: Harvard University Press, Third edition (1957)

Lévy-Bruhl, L. (1927). *The 'Soul' of the Primitive*, Chicago: Henry Regnery (1971); London: George Allen & Unwin (1966)

Maine, H. J. S. (1861). *Ancient Law*, London: J. Murray

Martin, D. A. (1962). 'The Denomination', *British Journal of Sociology*, Vol. 13, pp. 1-14

Marx, K. (1844). *Contribution to the Critique of Hegel's Philosophy of Right*, Reprinted in K. Marx and F. Engels: *On Religion*, Moscow: Foreign Language Publishing House

McKellar, P. (1957). *Imagination and Thinking*, London: Cohen and West

Mensching, G. 'The Masses, Folk Belief and Universal Religion', in Schneider, L. (ed.), *Religion, Culture and Society*,

London, New York: John Wiley (1964)

Merton, R. K. (1963). *Social Theory and Social Structure*, Glencoe, Ill.: Free Press

Miller, E. J. and Gwynne G. V. (1972). *A Life Apart*, London: Tavistock

Miller, E. J. and Rice, A. K. (1967). *Systems of Organisation*, London: Tavistock

Milner, M. (1956). 'The Sense in Non-sense', *New Era*, January 1956

Mol, H. (1976). *Identity and the Sacred*, Oxford: Basil Blackwell

Moreno, J. L. (1934). *Who Shall Survive?* Washington D.C.: Nervous and Mental Diseases Publishing Co.

Murray, G. (1925). *Five Stages of Greek Religion*, Oxford: Clarendon Press

Nadel, S. F. (1951). *The Foundations of Social Anthropology*, London: Cohen and West

Newman, E. (1937). *The Life of Richard Wagner 1848-1860*, New York: Knopf

Nietzsche, F. *The Genealogy of Morals*

Parens, H. and Saul, L. J. (1971). *Dependence in Man*, New York: International Universities Press

Pareto, V. (1916). *The Mind and Society*, English translation: New York: Harcourt, Brace & Co. (1935)

Plath, S. (1956). Letter of 24 February 1956, reprinted in Plath, A. S. (ed.), *Letters Home by Sylvia Plath*, London: Faber (1976)

Plato. *The Republic*

Poincaré, H. (1908). *Sciènce et Méthode*. Excerpt in Vernon, P. E. (ed.) (1970)

Popper, K. and Eccles, J. (1977). *The Self and its Brain*, Heidelberg, New York, London: Springer-Verlag

Radcliffe-Brown, A. R. (1952). *Structure and Function in Primitive Society*, Glencoe, Ill.: The Free Press; London: Cohen & West

Redfield, R. (1953). *The Primitive World and its Transformations*, USA: Cornell University Press

Reed, B. D. (1976). 'Organisational Role Analysis', in Cooper, C. L. (ed.), *Developing Social Skills in Managers*, London: Macmillan (1976)

Reed, B. D. and Palmer, B. W. M. (1972). *Introduction to Organisational Behaviour*, London: Grubb Institute (duplicated lectures)

Reed, B. D. and Palmer, B. W. M. (1972). 'The Local Church and its Environment', in E. J. Miller (ed.), *Task and Organisation*, London, New York: John Wiley (1976)

Rice, A. K. (1963). *The Enterprise and its Environment*, London: Tavistock

Richey, R. E. and Jones, D. G. (1974). *American Civil Religion*, New York: Harper & Row

Robertson, R. (ed.) (1969). *Sociology of Religion*, Harmondsworth: Penguin

Rycroft, C. (1962). 'Beyond the Reality Principle', in *Imagination and Reality*, London: Hogarth Press and Institute of Psycho-Analysis (1968)

Rycroft, C. (1968). *A Critical Dictionary of Psychoanalysis*, London: Nelson; Harmondsworth: Penguin (1972)

Slater, P. E. (1966). *Microcosm: Psychological and Religious Evolution in Groups*, New York, London: John Wiley

Stevenson, J. (ed.) (1957). *A New Eusebius*, London: SPCK

Tolstoy, L. N. (1884). *Memoirs of a Madman*, in *The Death of Iván Ilých and other stories*, London: Oxford University Press (first published 1935)

Tönnies, F. *Community and Society*, East Lansing, Michigan: Michigan State University Press (1957), first published as *Gemeinschaft und Gesellschaft* (1887)

Trist, E. L., Higgin, G. W., Murray, H. and Pollock, A. B. (1963). *Organisational Choice*, London: Tavistock

Troeltsch, E. (1931). *The Social Teaching of the Christian Churches*, London: Allen & Unwin

Turner, V. W. (1969). *The Ritual Process*, USA: Aldine; London: Routledge & Kegan Paul; Harmondsworth: Penguin (1974)

Turquet, P. M. (1974). 'Leadership: the Individual and the Group', in Gibbard, G. S., Hartman, J. J. and Mann, R. D. (eds.), *Analysis of Groups*, London: Jossey-Bass

Updike, J. (1968). *Couples*, London: Andre Deutsch

Vernon, P. E. (ed.) (1970). *Creativity*, Harmondsworth: Penguin

Vonnegut, K. (1967). *Player Piano*, London: Macmillan

Weber, M. (1922). *The Sociology of Religion*, Boston: Beacon Press (1964); London: Methuen (1965)

Wilson, B. R. (1963). 'A Typology of Sects', in Robertson, R. (1969)

Winnicott, D. W. (1958). *Collected Papers: Through Paediatrics to Psycho-analysis*, London: Tavistock

Winnicott, D. W. (1965). *The Maturational Process and the Facilitating Environment*, London: Hogarth Press and Institute of Psycho-Analysis

Winnicott, D. W. (1969). Private conversation with the writer. Extended notes in the possession of the Grubb Institute.

Index